Bennett & Hastings titles may be ordered through
booksellers or by contacting: bennetthastings@yahoo.com.

Bennett & Hastings' work on this book honors the
memory of Constance Ann Richards, whose love for animals
was ageless.

ISBN: 978-1-934733-51-6

B&H Bennett &
Hastings Publishing

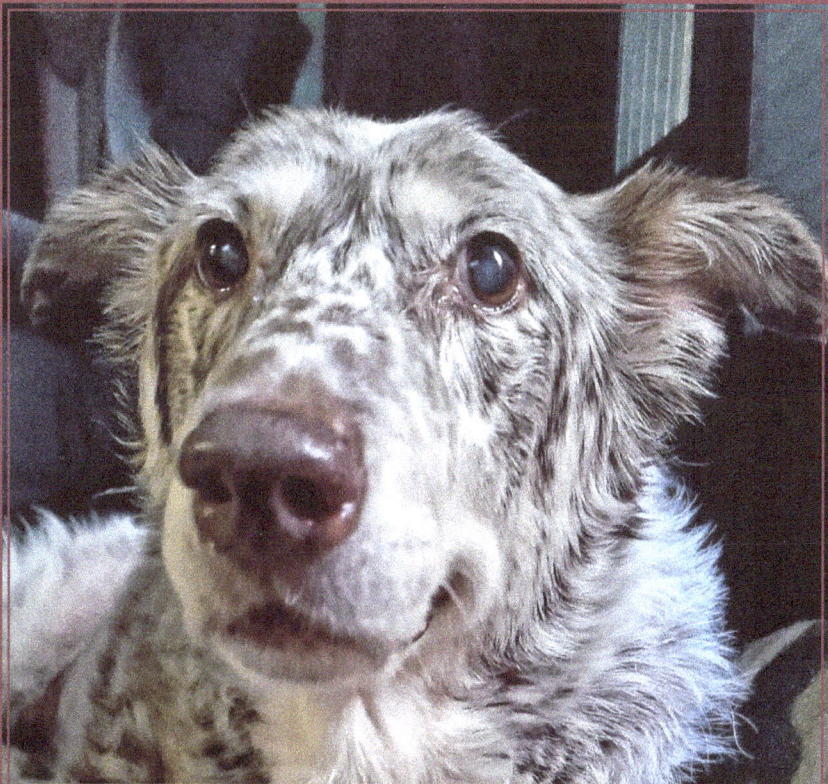

When I Grow Old, I will Wear Flowers

Thoughts about Senior Dogs

by Ardeth De Vries

Julie Austin Pet Photography Exp

Edie

Contents

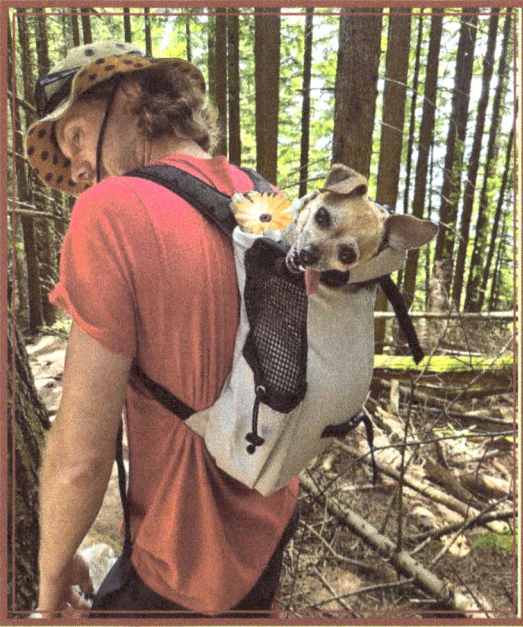

Ben and Aidy

This book is dedicated to people who value and love senior dogs, are willing to welcome them into their homes and hearts, and who give them opportunities to wear flowers.

Erica and Bob with Sophie and Bella

Juno

Acknowledgments

Thank you to the many dogs and people who provided information and inspiration for this book. Your photographs, words, and how you live your lives all honor senior dogs.

Original Photo Credits
(before I added flowers)

Julie Austin: Pearl (Cover) and (About Pearl, p. 156), Edie (Contents), Annie (Title Page), Harper, Josie and Cassie (Chapter 6, p. 45), Corrie (Chapter 10, p. 60), Tigger (Chapter 19, p. 101), Augustus (Chapter 26, p. 132), Cowbelle (Additional Resources), Moira (Additional Resources), Sadie (Additional Resources)

Mary Jo Adams: Java (Chapter 1, p. 16)

Julia N. Allen: Mama T (Chapter 9, p. 55)

Kim Barowicz: Buoy (Chapter 31, p. 153)

Celeste Bennett: Bella & Gunther (Additional Resources)

Beth Carroll: Welcome Home (Chapter 4, p. 32), Harry Pawter (Chapter 30, p. 148), Henry (Introduction, p. xv)

Rita Chan: Ruthie before and after (Chapter 21, p. 108)

Sara Chaney: Matt and Lucy (Chapter 11, p. 68)

Karen Corsini: Fiona (Chapter 5, p. 40)

Aaron Davis: Erica and Bob with Sophie and Bella (Dedication, p. vii), Bao (Chapter 7, p. 46), Gary and Oliver (Chapter 17, p. 93)

Dawn Ford: Aidy and Ben (Dedication, p. vii), Marvin (Chapter 10, p. 61)

Erin Grace: Emi (Chapter 18, p. 96)

Special thanks to foster families, staff, volunteers, and everyone else involved with Old Dog Haven, especially co-founders Judith and Lee Piper. What all of you do together to help senior dogs is nothing short of remarkable, and I'm proud to be a part of this organization.

Thank you to my publisher, Celeste Bennett, co-founder of Bennett and Hastings Publishers, LLC for believing in this book, providing invaluable expertise, excellent suggestions, and making sure that the book represents my vision. Celeste, you truly do have an animal heart.

Jane Sobel Klonsky
with Greta, Annie and Sammy

Foreword by Jane Sobel Klonsky

Everyone who has a relationship with a senior dog should own a copy of Ardeth's book *When I Grow Old I Will Wear Flowers: Thoughts About Senior Dogs* and keep it in a convenient place to grab for any and all answers to senior dog related questions, large or small. It's an "A to Z" encyclopedia of senior dogs, and every chapter is written clearly with knowledge and love and humor. There are many books out there that are about dogs. They entertain and feed a need but don't always expand our knowledge. Ardeth's book is different. She fills an important niche in this book genre. Her work will add something distinct, fresh and lasting that will stand out. In her new book, Ardeth combines her art of writing with her love for our best friends and delivers a wonderful experience.

About Jane Sobel Klonsky

Jane is an internationally known photographer/author who has photographed people, animals and places all over the world, but since 2012 her focus has been on people and the bond they have with their senior dogs. Jane is the photographer and founder of Unconditional Stories and the author of *Unconditional: Older Dogs. Deeper Love* (National Geographic 2016). She is also known for "Love Unleashed" (2017) created with her daughter, filmmaker Kacey Klonsky, as well as "Seniors, a dogumentary" (2020) created with filmmaker Gorman Bechard.

Jane is developing an international community of senior-dog lovers whose goal is to build a community and eventually be a home for friendships, support and information centered around our experiences and love for senior dogs. Recently, Jane and her daughter Kacey have started a mother-daughter photography business specializing in all things people, families, and their four-legged friends.

Introduction

You and I probably haven't actually met, but I've seen you walking your dog. I've seen you with your dog at the vet clinic. I've seen you at the animal shelter looking at the dogs needing homes. I've seen you with your dog at a picnic with other people and dogs. I've seen you in your back yard playing geriatric fetch with your dog as I walk past your house. I've imagined you in your home sitting on the couch watching television with your dog. I've seen you in the bookstore looking at the title of this book. Now we'll actually meet, and I'd like to offer a few thoughts about senior dogs in this book.

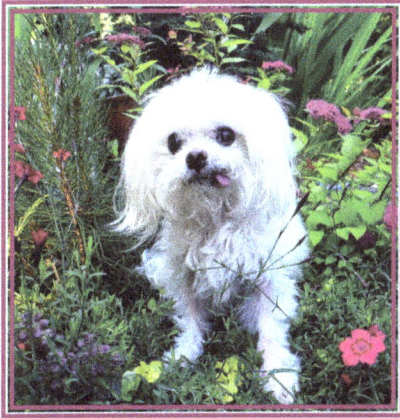

Henry

When I Grow Old I Will Wear Flowers: Thoughts About Senior Dogs is rather like a buffet; there's a bit of everything to sample. I'm not presenting you with an in-depth look at any one topic, but rather asking you to think about many different topics relating to senior dogs regardless of your situation; you may be living with a senior dog that has been with you for years, or you may be interested in adopting or fostering a senior dog. Let's start there, but first I'd like you to think about why some senior dogs end up in shelters.

Java

Chapter 1

Why Do Some Senior Dogs
End Up in Shelters?

*Their value in the eyes of others has diminished,
and they've become expendable.*

That's a good question, and there are several answers, some of which might surprise you. Knowing the why behind the thousands of homeless senior dogs living in shelters probably isn't particularly helpful, but I just felt you should know the facts so you understand what many senior dogs have experienced. Hopefully you may consider adopting a senior dog from a shelter. I've walked dogs at our local shelter for over 20 years, and I've seen many dogs from the scenarios listed below:

- Many senior dogs that end up in shelters were cherished companions of elderly people who died or had to move into a care facility that won't allow dogs. One day the dog is lounging on a couch, or sitting on his person's lap, and then all of a sudden he finds himself in a cage surrounded by barking dogs. There wasn't any kind of plan in place to see to the needs of the dog if life circumstances changed, and the family either won't take the dog or there is no family to assume responsibility for the dog.

- Economic hardships cause a family to lose their home, and the dog becomes homeless too.

- People divorce and neither person wants the dog.

- Children are born, and the senior dog loses the attention of the family.

- The senior dog isn't able to tolerate young children because of their energy level, or the parents just don't want one more responsibility.

- Animal Control Involvement:

- Dogs are taken from hoarders.

- Dogs are removed from homes because of neglect and/or abuse.

- Puppy mills are raided by authorities and the elderly dogs birthing them are sent to shelters.

- Dogs are brought to shelters as strays by Animal Control with no history at all. Many are in terrible shape, but some are relatively healthy. Many of these "strays" are found by the side of the road, often injured. Others are found wandering in neighborhoods. (I must say here that I think the term "stray" is absurd. Dogs don't just fall from the sky. They become stray dogs because no one is looking for them.)

- Dogs are abandoned in empty houses.

- Neighbors intervene and contact Animal Control on behalf of a neglected dog.

- People bring dogs to shelters claiming they're strays so they don't have to pay a surrender fee.

- Former show dogs are no longer useful, and are brought to shelters to be euthanized.

- People move away, and don't want to take the dog with them for various reasons.

- The dog has health issues the family doesn't want to deal with, either for financial reasons or because they just don't want to be bothered with a sick dog.

- People say they have no time for the dog.

- The dog is brought to a shelter by the dog's human companion to be euthanized.

- The dog has become incontinent and rather than taking the dog to a vet to determine the problem, the dog's people bring the dog to a shelter ... in many cases without telling the shelter the real reason they're surrendering the dog.

- Senior dogs are traded in for puppies.

In a later chapter, I talk about **planning ahead** because the whole shelter experience and/or many of the above mentioned situations can be prevented by planning for the care of a senior dog before life circumstances change. Sadly, many people don't plan ahead, so the bottom line is the same for all of the senior dogs in shelters represented by the above list: no one wants them. Their value in the eyes of others has diminished, and they've become expendable.

And yes, I know you feel angry about some of the reasons given above, but please don't waste your energy thinking about the actions of people who abandon senior dogs. I'd like to tell you that people can be educated to think differently about bringing a senior dog to a shelter, but for many people dogs are possessions (as they are considered in the eyes of the law) and no amount of education is going to change that perception. Instead, focus on the dogs. Adopt a senior dog from a shelter. Or, if you're unable to adopt, visit your local shelter and become a volunteer. Shelters do what they can to help all dogs in residence (especially senior dogs) but volunteers are always welcome. You could walk dogs, or just hang out with them and let them know you care about them. Let them know they have value.

Chapter 2

Adopting or Fostering a Senior Dog

Adopting me proves that it's never too late for happiness. Maybe for both of us.

If you're thinking about adopting a senior dog you can visit your local shelter, or you can check rescue organizations in your area to see if they have any senior dogs that might be available for adoption. (See the Resources listed by state at the end of this book.)

Why adopt a senior dog? I'm going to give you 10 reasons why you should adopt a senior dog from a dog's point of view. Think of me as an interpreter; I've been around senior dogs for 55 years so I think I know pretty well how they feel:

1) I don't like how it feels to be homeless. To understand my feelings a bit, think about what it would be like to be a homeless person. Now, extend that thought and imagine how you would feel if you were an abandoned, homeless senior citizen. Life as you knew it before you became homeless is a memory that has become barely a whisper in your mind. You're confused, sad, afraid, perhaps not healthy, and no one wants you. You've lived your life in the best way you know how, but now your value has so diminished in the eyes of others that you've become expendable. That's how I feel.

2) I'm very adaptable and resilient. You might think that because I'm older I might be set in my ways, but actually that's not true. I can adapt to a new situation, and what I've been through has made me resilient and ready for a sec-

ond chance at happiness. I can learn whatever you have to teach me and, to return the favor, maybe I could teach you a thing or two as well.

3) My wild and crazy puppy days are over, and I'm pretty calm and laid back most of the time. I say most of the time because there are things like walks, rides, treats, and maybe even toys that get me excited and happy. I may be older but there's a lot I can still enjoy. It's all about simple pleasures.

4) On a practical level, I understand that I'm supposed to go outside to do my business, and I know about walking on a leash. No training required.

5) I may be a little unsure of myself right now because I'm in a shelter, but my sense of who I am is still intact, just ready to emerge again when I feel more secure and less stressed.

6) If you're older too maybe we can reverse the clock a bit and grow younger together.

7) I'm really big on living in the moment and enjoying one day at a time. We could do that together.

8) One of my very favorite things is being near someone who loves me. I'm a great cuddler. I don't care what TV shows you watch, although I am partial to shows about dogs. I'd just like to be snuggling on the couch with you.

9) I can show you how to meet life's challenges with grace and optimism.

10) Adopting me proves that it's never too late for happiness. Maybe for both of us.

❀ ❀ ❀

If adopting a senior dog isn't a financial possibility for you, perhaps you might like to foster a senior dog. Contact rescue groups in your area: see if they need fosters and how much they're willing to help with expenses.

If you live in Western Washington, contact Old Dog Haven **(www.olddoghaven.org)** for fostering opportunities. I could write a book about Old Dog Haven. (Oh wait ... I already have: *Old Dog Haven: Every Old Dog Has a Story to Tell.)* Old Dog Haven provides permanent foster homes for unadoptable senior dogs, eight years and older. Dogs live in private homes as members of families who love them and care for them the rest of their lives. All veterinary expenses are paid for by Old Dog Haven.

You'll hear me talk about Old Dog Haven quite often in the coming pages because I've been involved with this amazing organization for 18 years.

❀

I could tell you what it's like to foster, but I think I'll let you hear from some of Old Dog Haven's foster families instead:

- "My pledge to each dog that crosses my threshold is simple: You are wanted. You are safe. You will not die alone. You will not be forgotten."

- "Quality of life centers all our actions for the seniors in our care, and nothing improves the quality of life as much as love."

Bev and Duke

- "We consider what we do and the caretaking of souls to be a gift."

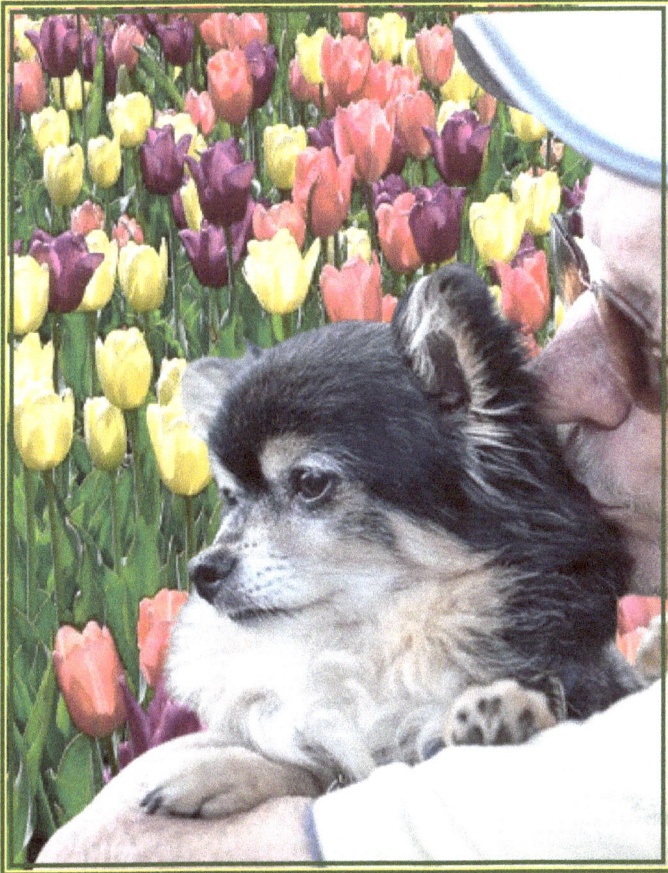

Aaron and Nikki

▪ "It's changed our life. It's changed how we look at life. It's changed how we live our life."

Zelda

Chapter 3

Budgeting for your Senior Dog

It's important not to make a lifetime commitment to a dog if you can't afford the care.

I've mentioned that some senior dogs end up in shelters because people can't afford to care for them, so I'd like to talk a bit about what kinds of expenses you'll incur if you adopt a senior dog. I don't want you to adopt a dog and then find out later that you don't have the money to care for his medical needs. Within this context I find that it's a good idea to establish a "dog care fund" that you can access each month. That way, when you need a vet visit for your dog the money is available.

I wish I could give you exact numbers, but veterinary costs across the country vary so much it isn't really possible to do that with any degree of accuracy. Even within certain states and cities the costs aren't always consistent. And, you'll find that prices vary at vet clinics within specific cities. (To test this statement I checked with six different vets within one city and came up with six different prices for a nail trim, ranging from free to $100.)

Here's a website that might help you with current vet costs:

https://www.betterpet.com>dog-ownership-costs

Following are some of the expenses you can expect to have if you adopt a senior dog:

1) **Adoption fee**—one time only

2) **Microchip**—one time only unless you move and need to update your contact information

3) **Dental**—teeth should be checked <u>once a year</u> and often a dental (cleaning, extractions) can take place at that time. If you keep up with teeth care the cost won't escalate because of the amount of work that needs to be done. If you adopt a dog that hasn't had any kind of dental care for years you're liable to pay big bucks for that first dental. Also, because your dog is a senior the vet will want to run a blood test to be sure your dog can handle the anesthesia, which is always a risk with a senior dog. To help, you can brush your dog's teeth on a regular basis.

4) **Grooming**—This could be a no cost item if your dog is short-haired and you're willing to bathe and brush him on a regular basis. Dogs with longer hair require grooming more often (<u>maybe once a month</u>) and you can do this too if you buy a pair of clippers designed for dogs and you have a bath tub or large sink. If you'd rather use a professional groomer, that's great but **be sure that the groomer either specializes in senior dogs or comes highly recommended by other people who have senior dogs.**

5) **Nail trim**—Toe nails need to be trimmed on a regular basis (<u>maybe once a month</u>) so your dog's ability to walk won't be impacted by long nails. You can do this yourself, or it can be done as part of a vet or groomer visit. This isn't a big ticket item in terms of cost if you'd rather have someone else do it. (I used to trim my dogs' nails myself, but my current group of dogs all seem to be competing for the "Biggest Drama Queen" title, and they keep saying, "I Need My Toe Nails to Tap Dance: Don't Touch Them," so I have a very

patient vet technician do it when I bring them in for an appointment.

6) **Vaccinations**—When you first bring your dog to the vet for his initial appointment the vet will establish a vaccination schedule specifically for your dog. The vet will often send reminders when vaccinations are due (every one-three years).

7) **Flea, heartworm, tick prevention**—Pills are mostly typically used here and are available at your vet clinic or you can order them online. Ask your vet which medication is best for your dog (usually once a month).

8) **A Blood test** should be done once a year. Your dog may seem healthy, but many problems common to senior dogs (kidney function, heart failure, liver disease) may not present symptoms until your dog become seriously ill, so a yearly blood test is an excellent diagnostic tool. Early detection of disease through blood work offers more effective and less costly treatment options.

9) **Urinalysis**—every six months to check for urinary tract infections, bladder stones, kidney failure, diabetes and many other diseases.

10) **Emergency vet visits**—These are those middle-of-the-night vet visits you never want to have, yet you'll probably be doing this trip at least once with your dog. The cost here could really be high depending on whether hospitalization or surgery is required.

11) **Illness or injury requiring treatment**—This is one of those categories that will really vary in terms of cost, depending on what's required in terms of treatment.

12) **Leash, harness, collar, bedding, toys**—Here's where you can spend a lot of money, or very little, depending on how often you want to change these items. Check with your local thrift store to see it they have what you need at a lower cost. Also, if your dog is incontinent and you're using pee pads, check local thrift stores, shelters, and rescue groups for assistance here.

13) **Pet Sitting, Walking, Boarding**—This category may not be relevant for everyone, but if you need any of these services they can be pricey depending on what you require. Your vet will be an excellent resource here in terms of recommendations.

14) **Travel**—If you like to travel with your dog there are many pet-friendly places to stay but they're often more expensive than regular accommodations. (If you have an RV this is the best possible solution.)

15) **Diagnostic Imaging**—includes radiographs (x-rays), ultrasound, MRIs and CT scans, all of which are used as diagnostic tools to collect information about your dog's health. The vast majority of imaging is non-invasive and completely painless. If any of these are required, your vet will advise you. And yes, they're expensive.

16) **Pet Insurance**—Pet insurance is an optional expense that will probably cost between $25-30 per month depending on what kind of coverage you require.

I know this seems like a long list, and I've probably forgotten a few things, but I just wanted to give you an idea about the kinds of expenses you might incur if you have a senior dog so you can budget accordingly. It's important not to make a lifetime commitment to a dog if you can't afford the care.

Angel   Bernie   Shalom   Henry   Ellie   Chase   Talla   Sassy

Welcome Home!

Chapter 4

Welcoming a New Dog into your Home

Remind yourself that older dogs are amazingly resilient and have the ability to adapt very quickly to new situations.

If you're thinking about adopting or fostering an older dog I have a few thoughts about a welcoming routine that you might find helpful, so I'll just pass them on for your consideration. Just use what makes sense for your situation.

I'm going to call your new dog Andy just so I don't have to keep saying "the new dog."

Manage your expectations before Andy arrives.

1) Your home will most likely be a big change for Andy if he found himself in a shelter or perhaps has been living in a temporary home because his person has died or some life-changing circumstance has caused him to become homeless. Regardless of background, Andy may need time to adjust to his new home. Don't expect him to instantly be comfortable and secure.

2) Be optimistic and excited rather than apprehensive about welcoming Andy. Dogs are intuitive, and they process everything emotionally so your attitude and energy will be picked up by Andy when you meet him.

3) Understand that whatever you may have been told about Andy in terms of behavior and personality may not neces-

sarily be true in your home. This is especially relevant if he's coming directly from a shelter. Shelters are very stressful places, especially for older dogs, and stress contributes directly to a dog's behavior and personality while he's at the shelter. Once in a home you may see a totally different dog.

4) If Andy is grieving for his person, he may likely be withdrawn and sad when he arrives. That will change in time with your help.

5) Understand that dogs, like people, have developed habits, routines and "this is what I'm used to" stuff over the years that may linger for a while in a new home. Resolve to be patient with Andy as he adjusts to his new life.

6) If Andy is coming to you from a home rather than a shelter I'd suggest you make arrangements to pick him up at some neutral place rather than having his people bring him to you. Seeing the people who brought him to you drive away from your house without him will be very hard on Andy, especially if he's confused and apprehensive. Also, a neutral place will be easier for Andy rather than you taking him away from his home.

7) If you have young children, and they're not used to having an older dog around make sure you talk to them about how they need to be gentle with Andy and respectful of him because he's older.

8) If you're adopting/fostering Andy as a way to honor the memory of another senior dog companion that is no longer physically with you, don't expect Andy to be that dog. Resolve to allow Andy to be the dog he is without expecting him to be just like your other dog.

The Welcoming: Meeting Your Other Dogs

1) If you have another dog and he tends to be territorial, it's best to let the dogs meet in a neutral place (not in your yard or home). It's often good to just put them on leashes and take them for a walk together. If you have more than one dog, have a family member help.

2) If your dog is good with other dogs, it works well to let them meet without leashes in a very safe, fenced spot outside—not too small—leave room for maneuvering. Don't worry if they play-skirmish a bit; they have to work out what their relationship is to each other. Try to ignore them and not referee. If you have a fenced yard, when you arrive home let Andy into your yard, remove his leash, and then bring your other dog out to meet him. If you have more than one dog, bring the dogs out one at a time. Your other dogs should be off-leash too. Allow the dogs to explore the yard and get acquainted without being pushy. They'll do fine together if you just let them meet and greet in their own way. You can't choreograph this dance. Just stand back and smile.

3) Once the initial introductions are made, invite Andy into the house and let him explore. You don't need to be a tour guide; he'll find the water bowl and the dog beds.

4) If you have a doggie door, begin the process of teaching Andy how to use it. In a perfect world your other dogs may do this for you. How long it takes Andy to use the doggie door is a crapshoot; I've had dogs catch on right away, but sometimes it takes days or weeks. With dogs that don't see well, using the doggie door may never happen. Again, just be patient. But make sure Andy knows that he needs to go outside to do his business. Senior dogs are generally

housebroken so this shouldn't be a problem unless the dog is coming right from a shelter, in which case you may have to do some re-teaching about bathroom etiquette.

5) Sit down, relax and just let Andy get used to his new home. Don't follow him around or be pushy about wanting him to sit near you, on your lap or be close to you. If you've bailed him out of the shelter he may do all of that right away because you rescued him and he'll be your Velcro dog, but maybe it'll take time.

6) When it's time for bed, allow Andy to sleep wherever is comfortable for him. Make sure he has his own bed or he knows he's welcome on your bed if you like your dogs to sleep with you. Whatever you do, it's very important that you don't isolate him from you or the rest of your family (including other dogs). He needs to feel like he's part of the family right from the beginning.

Settling In

1) Feed Andy small amounts for the first day or two, using any food that came with him, gradually mixing in whatever you choose to feed. If he doesn't eat much right away or even vomits from nerves, don't panic. Feed him well away from the others, and don't offer treats for a couple of days. Don't encourage excited play with toys, or offer chewies close to the other dogs until the pecking order has settled.

2) Avoid unnecessary stress until Andy feels safe with you. Wait a couple of days to begin bathing and grooming (unless he smells so awful a bath is really necessary.) If he's very matted, cut away the worst of the mats and trim away from his eyes. Try not to have too many visitors or take him to strange places for the first week.

3) What takes patience is letting Andy get used to a new routine, showing him what's expected without putting too much pressure on him. Don't hover. Let him relax and work his way into the family. Don't be surprised if he sleeps a lot once he relaxes—especially if he came from a shelter. He's probably exhausted.

4) For a smooth adjustment, pay a more than usual amount of attention to the resident dogs if you have other dogs. You need to reassures the other dogs that Andy hasn't come to replace them in any way. Try to keep life the same for them.

5) Remember that each of the dogs in your family may have some special activities or time with you. Don't change that. As long as each dog gets his own special attention all will be well.

6) If your other dogs are rescue dogs too, they'll understand that Andy needs to be there. They haven't forgotten their early days when they were first rescued and they understand the need to be accepted and loved.

Ok, that's enough. Just use whatever seems right for you and your situation. Remind yourself that older dogs are amazingly resilient and have the ability to adapt very quickly to new situations. Andy will know that living with you is an opportunity to be a happy dog, and he'll be ready and willing to become valued, respected and a well-loved member of your family.

Maddie Mae

Chapter 5

Babies, Small Children, and Senior Dogs

*Regardless of the size of the dog, young children need
to be taught how to interact with older dogs*

Two songs—"Teach Your Children" (Crosby, Stills and Nash) and "Respect" (Aretha Franklin)—are going through my head right now as I think about what I want to say in this chapter.

I've already mentioned that people often bring senior dogs to the shelter because the children aren't interacting well with the dog. The #2 reason given by people who contact Old Dog Haven asking for help to re-home their senior dog is that the dog is having problems with small children and/or the baby in the house. Old Dog Haven receives these requests multiple times a day—every day.

Senior dogs—like many senior people—often have little tolerance for loud noises, lots of commotion, and change. Also, the reaction time of a dog slows as he ages, and if you add loss of vision, hearing or mobility, a senior dog often becomes a target for small children and many times he will feel vulnerable. Small dogs seem to have a harder time than bigger dogs because it's easy for small children to pick them up and haul them around, but it's the bigger dogs that get laid on and pulled on. If a child gets the "wrong" spot when he pulls on a dog because the dog is sore from arthritis or the child startles the dog (deaf dog sleeping), it could be the time the dog reacts and bites.

Regardless of the size of the dog, young children need to be taught how to interact with older dogs. You wouldn't let your young child chase or pull on your grandmother, would you? And, using the same comparison, you wouldn't give your child away if he bit Grandpa, would you? It's very important for parents to take the time to teach their children to be kind and respectful to the family dog.

And then there's the issue of babies and old dogs. Babies can be noisy. If a dog is already nervous or has issues with change, having a baby in the house will probably be hard on him. This is something parents need to think about before deciding to have a baby or adopting/fostering a dog if they have a baby. Parents need to be honest with themselves about whether they (and the dog) can handle the dog/baby experience. It's far better to find the dog a home before he has a bad experience (and while he's a little younger) because once the dog has bitten the baby/toddler he will be extremely hard to rehome and may have to go through a quarantine period. Or, worst case scenario—the dog may be euthanized.

Fiona

Parents are responsible for making sure both baby and dog are safe at all times. Even if the dog is fine until the baby starts crawling, once that baby is mobile, parents need to be sure the baby and the dog interact appropriately. That takes monitoring.

Here are some of the comments we hear all the time from people who contact Old Dog Haven asking us to help them re-home their senior dog:

- "My dog was my first baby, but now I have a real baby."

- "The dog was fine until the baby came home and she started crying."

- "We've moved the dog into the garage because of the baby, and now the dog is anxious and barks all the time."

- "The dog bit the crawling baby twice."

- "The dog snapped at the kids because they were chasing him and laying all over him."

- "With the kids and my job, caring for the dog is just too much—I can't handle it all."

Senior dogs can live very successfully with babies and/or small children BUT parents need to step up and teach their children to be kind and respectful to the dog, and parents need to carefully monitor the interaction between the dog and the children. It's actually very healthy for children to live with dogs, not only because of what the dog can teach the child, but what the child can learn about empathy, compassion, and a sense of responsibility if parents are willing to use the child's experiences with the dog as teachable moments and to encourage positive interaction.

Parents: Please don't let your senior dog end up in a shelter just because you didn't take time to teach your children to be kind and respectful to the dog.

Chapter 6

Dog Roles

Because dogs process everything emotionally they feel their connections with other dogs, and often those connections aren't influenced by experience.

I've been thinking about how people interact with each other, which—predictably—leads me to think about dogs and how they interact with each other. First, let's talk about people.

Human-to-human interaction is largely driven by relationships. You probably wouldn't talk to your grandmother in the same way you converse with your teenage son, nor would you share personal information with the checker at Safeway in the same way you do with your best friend. Our relationships are based on experiences—our history with other people—and those experiences color our interactions.

Our interactions are also driven by common causes. You may not know all of the people who are involved in a particular organization—like Old Dog Haven for example—but because you have a common bond with them based on relationships with senior dogs, your interactions with them are informed by that shared belief in the dignity and value of senior dogs.

So, what about dogs? What causes them to interact with each other in certain, sometimes very specific, ways? Do their experiences influence their interactions too? Probably yes in some cases, but what about the interactions that don't seem based on experience?

Here's an example: My friend Joey—off on another adventure now—came to live with me at a time when there were three other dogs in residence. Joey hadn't met any of these other dogs before he came home from the shelter with me, but within a matter of hours I watched him interact in a different way with each dog. He saw Harper as his dad—even though he was older than Harper. I watched him defer to Harper, follow his lead, and generally be very "son-like" with him. Then there was his interaction with Molly; Joey was polite with her, as she was with him, but there wasn't really much of a connection between them. Acquaintances maybe. And Fitz. Fitz was damaged in many ways. I watched Joey tune in to the insecurity and sadness that Fitz carried around with him, and it was as if Joey wrapped his paws around Fitz emotionally, and very rarely left his side.

You may be wondering if Joey's experiences with other dogs played a part in his interactions with Harper, Molly, and Fitz but Joey was an only dog, and he had lived with one person for all of his ten years. His human was very reclusive and never socialized Joey with other dogs. When his person died, Joey was brought to the shelter and didn't interact with other dogs at all.

I have another example for you: Many years ago, Duncan lived with me along with two other dogs. Duncan was an old dog and had mobility issues. When Henry (also a dog) came to live with us, he immediately related to Duncan as a grandpa. I carried Duncan down the stairs most of the time, but sometimes he wanted to try on his own. One day Duncan started down the stairs, and Henry was immediately at his side. Duncan had the wall on one side, and Henry on the other side supporting him. Together they went down the stairs, and Henry never let Duncan fall. Not once. Henry shared Duncan's bed, he stood next to him while he ate, and in short ... Duncan had his own personal support dog.

Here's what I think: Because dogs process everything emotionally they feel their connections with other dogs, and often those connections aren't influenced by experience. Dogs relate to each other in ways that are based on need and a kind of intuitive understanding. Watch your own dogs, and you'll see that there are interesting dynamics going on as they interact with each other. You'll see friends, relatives, and casual acquaintances dancing to music only they can hear. You'll see playfulness, aloofness, trust, and even total disinterest as they do their dance with each other.

So, what's the point here? I just find it interesting to notice how dogs interact with each other. I guess part of my fascination has to do with the fact that dogs cut to the chase, and they move right past preconceived ideas and just go with what they feel as they live their lives. Maybe another lesson we could learn.

Josie, Harper and Cassie

Bao

Chapter 7

How to Help a Grieving Dog

Grieving is his way to honor his friend—human or animal—just as it is with people, so allow him the time and space to do that.

In another chapter I'll talk about productive grieving for people who are mourning the loss of an animal friend, but right now I want to talk about helping a dog—especially a senior dog—that is grieving. This chapter may be especially relevant for those of you who are fostering or who have adopted an older dog that has experienced loss in his life. Or, if you have a dog that is mourning the death of an animal friend, this chapter will explain a grieving process that goes on that I'd like you to consider.

You probably know this, but to restate the obvious, dogs grieve too. In fact, because dogs process everything emotionally and intuitively, their grieving process is often very difficult for them. Their sense of loss is so profoundly emotional.

I suppose I should talk first about signs that may indicate that your dog is grieving. Each dog processes a sense of loss differently (as do people) so you may not see all of these signs—in fact, you may see the opposite of what I'm listing here:

- loss of appetite
- lethargy and depression
- wakefulness—or the opposite—sleeping more than usual

- accidents in the house

- acting up, i.e. behavior issues

- separation anxiety

- vocalizations—not necessarily barking, but howling, whimpering and whining

- personality changes (This seems especially true if the dog is grieving for another animal and he's not sure what his role is now that his friend is gone.)

As always, I recommend that you see a vet to be sure whatever symptoms are appearing aren't related to a physical problem. If the problem isn't physical, then here are a few thoughts about how you can help:

1) Recognize that your dog may be grieving. It's very important that you honor and respect what your canine friend is going through by letting him know you understand and are there for him.

2) Look after your dog's physical needs. It's important that he's healthy so he feels strong enough to grieve. You also need to be aware of the fact that prolonged grieving can often cause physical problems that need to be addressed. As with people, the mental, emotional and physical facets of a dog are all connected.

3) Do whatever you can to bond with him, i.e. special outings, letting him sleep on the bed with you, snuggle time on the couch, special healthy treats, etc.

4) Stick to a routine that will help him feel secure. Whatever loss he's experienced has caused him to feel like he doesn't know what to expect any more, and it's your job to reassure him that all is well by being consistent.

5) Add a bit more exercise and stimulation to his life. The physical activity will help him feel more settled in his feelings.

6) Don't be a helicopter friend. Hovering and playing the "you poor baby" game with a dog that is grieving only intensifies the grief and isn't helpful. You can certainly be sympathetic, but it's better to say, "You're ok. I'm here for you," than to feel sorry for him in any kind of dramatic way.

7) If your dog is experiencing grief because of the loss of an animal companion be careful about introducing a new dog into the family right away. I can't tell you how long to wait because each situation is different, but don't expect that getting him a new friend immediately will work miracles. Put yourself in his place: if a friend, family member, partner or spouse dies, you don't rush out right away and find another person to replace the one who died. You need time to process your grief. Also, if you're going to welcome another dog into your home and heart, I'd suggest you have your grieving friend help you choose the dog.

8) If your dog (and in this case it's probably a new dog to you) is grieving because his person died or went into assisted living, or perhaps his people divorced, moved, or are unable to care for him for whatever reason, it's important that you don't try to replace that person (or people) but instead form a new relationship with your dog. Again, I'll ask you to relate to a people situation: if you begin a relationship

with a person who is grieving for someone who doesn't physically exist in their life any longer, you wouldn't try to replace that person would you? Ideally, you would honor the role the person who is no longer there played in the life of your significant other or friend, and then you'd move on together.

9) Helping a dog grieve is tricky because dogs live in the moment so they're very capable and willing to be fully present in their lives. But, because time is a relative concept in the life of a dog sometimes the moments aren't always right now but yesterday, or last week, or even last month. The imprints of the past often stay with them. It's up to you to help them erase the sadness and replace it with happy moments. The only way to bring them out of their sadness is to let the light in. Help your dog make new memories.

10) Finally, be patient. It make take weeks, or even months for your dog to emerge from grief. Just hang in there and honor the process by allowing him to make sense of it all in his own time with your help. Grieving is his way to honor his friend—human or animal—just as it is with people, so allow him the time and space to do that. One thing you have going for you here is that dogs are willing to trust you to help them trade sadness for happiness. They want to be well—on all levels—so grieving isn't something they enjoy or want to prolong for any length of time.

Chapter 8

Teaching a Senior Human New Tricks

My dogs think they're doing me a favor by reminding me about my role in their lives. "It's for your own good" is a cartoon bubble I see over their heads quite often.

Elliott

My dogs and I have a great system worked out in terms of our roles in the household as well as our various responsibilities. Because my dogs are all seniors they've spent years perfecting their routines and, as all dogs that have come to me before them, they've trained me very well. Here's our version of teamwork and their ability to teach an old human new tricks:

- Their jobs are to tip over the garbage can in the kitchen as well as the wastebaskets in the office, and my job is to clean up the mess. When I talk to them about this behavior they insist that I don't have enough to do, and they're just making sure I keep busy. They always forget to mention that there might be cracker or cookie wrappers in the wastebasket.

• When I'm out in the yard doing poop patrol they often follow me outside, and just to be sure the activity is worthwhile they poop in the area I've just scooped because they want me to understand that they know why I'm there, and that my job is necessary.

• When we're walking on the beach they help me to remember their names, which they think is necessary because often I call them "Don't Eat That, " or "Leave It," or "Put That Down."

• When we're riding in the truck they allow me to sit in the driver's seat because they don't drive, but they're very careful to direct me to Starbucks, and if I don't come out with a whipped cream treat in my hand they show off their best pouting faces and threaten to call Animal Control to complain about being neglected.

• Most of them sleep on the bed with me at night, and they're very generous about allowing me a few inches on the side of the bed. If I dare to take up too much room they remind me that I'm a guest on their bed.

• Jack, our Wildlife Warden, is very vocal about warning us about the presence of monsters (like squirrels, deer, and bunnies) in the yard. He barks, I go out and call him inside, he goes out the other door, barks, I call him inside …. Meanwhile the other dogs have joined the barking, and we have a chorus instead of a solo. Even little Soren, who can't quite manage the doggie door because he's blind, joins the chorus—only he makes sure I open the sliding door—which is next to the doggie door—for him. It's a dance we do very well together, and Jack is always proud of himself because he's doing his job so well, and he doesn't understand why I complain about my job.

. My dogs are magicians when it's time for baths and haircuts. They're very good at the "Now you see me, now you don't" trick when I even think about starting the bathing process. I don't have to say anything out loud. They just know. They endure the whole ordeal pretty gracefully in a passive-aggressive sort of way, which means that I get wetter than they do, and most of their hair is transferred to my clothes rather than the floor when I get to the haircut stage of the grooming process.

. They're training me to be patient when waiting for them to respond to my call. When it's time to leave the beach or park, and I call them to the truck, I know there will be a certain amount of dawdling on the way because they want me to learn how to wait for them and to understand that they'll come when they're ready.

. Zuleia, one of our new dogs, has discovered the toy basket, and she's teaching us to throw the toy and admire her fetching abilities. She's particularly fond of squeaky toys, and she runs around the house with the toy in her mouth making unpleasant noises. When I remind her that she's a senior and not a puppy she mutters something about age being just a number, and she gives me the stink eye. We're considering ear plugs, and the other dogs are thinking about packing their bags.

My dogs think they're doing me a favor by reminding me about my role in their lives. "It's for your own good" is a cartoon bubble I see over their heads quite often. Could be, but why does the word "smug" come to mind when I see the expressions on their faces?

Chapter 9

Differently-Abled Senior Dogs

Differently-abled senior dogs view life with a simplicity and purity of emotion that we would be wise to emulate when it comes to how we see them.

Mama-T

I was once asked to write an article for the Washington Animal Control Association newsletter about caring for companion animals that are disabled, and I thought this topic might be of interest to you because of my overall perception regarding disabilities.

Mama-T was found just off a busy I-5 interchange and brought to a shelter by a Good Samaritan. Mama-T ("T" for tripod) couldn't walk very far or very fast because her left front leg was amputated years ago, and her overworked right front leg tired very quickly. She just didn't have the ability to escape from a vehicle on her own, so she was probably dumped in a parking lot near the highway.

She'd been micro-chipped about 12 years ago, and the shelter was able to reach the person with whom she lived, but that person had given Mama-T away before moving to another state.

The shelter contacted Old Dog Haven for help, and this loving old girl enjoyed two years in her Final Refuge forever home before her body completely failed her. She received treatment for a chronic ear infection, severe arthritis in both knees (cruciate ligament rupture), miscellaneous skin growths, and generalized itching and flaky skin–all treatable and all managed to keep her healthy and happy!

Mama-T loved to go outside, and really loved to go for walks. Thanks to the generosity of Old Dog Haven donors, Mama-T had a 4-wheeled cart that she used to get out and about in while staying balanced and safe. When not out hot-rodding in her fancy rig, Mama-T just loved to lay in the sun and chase water from the hose while her mom watered the flowers.

Eventually her cart was adorned with a hot pink supplies pouch at the rear, flashing white headlights, and flashing red taillights. She adored people and would head straight over to anyone who would stop and talk to her.

Thanks to Old Dog Haven donors, Mama-T was provided with two years of mobility to get out around the neighborhood and meet many new friends. She loved running in her cart and sometimes ran about two miles a day.

I'm also thinking about the many dogs that have lived with me who were blind and/or deaf. Don't hesitate about adopting or fostering a blind or deaf dog. Dogs that can't see or hear have an amazing ability to navigate around using what I call their "radar." Yes, for a dog to adjust from being sighted to blind, or from hearing well to being completely deaf requires some time, but with your help, blind and deaf dogs can live very happy lives.

Within this context, I need to tell you about my friend, Sally. Sally was a shelter dog that was completely blind and deaf when she came to the shelter as a "stray." Sally's radar was the best I've ever seen, and she showed a confidence rarely seen in any shelter dog—with or without vision and hearing. Sally always knew where she was: she actually ran without hesitation in the open space of the play yard. When anyone came near her she sensed their presence, and walked right over to them, and when I took her for walks, she walked right out in front of me.

The word "disabled" often conjures up all kinds of thoughts and feelings which aren't necessary or productive, especially when it comes to our perception of dogs that are functioning in a way that is different than other dogs. Instead of thinking about them as disabled just because they can't see, hear, are missing limbs, or have some other perceived disability, why not think about your dog as being differently-abled?

If you're caring for a differently-abled dog here are a few thoughts that might be helpful to you:

- Understand that your dog is very willing and able to learn how to function without using eyes or ears if those are the issues that concern you. With your patience and guidance blind and deaf dogs do very well.

- If mobility is the problem, know that there are many websites that offer support, assistance and information about carts or other related products. Just type in "Pets with Disabilities" in your search engine and you'll be pleasantly surprised how much support is out there.

Differently-abled senior dogs:

- make every effort to do what they can to their maximum potential,

- have more patience than humans will ever have in the same situation,

- don't worry about their needs being taken care of; they know we'll do that,

- need our acceptance to honor them as they are, not as we wish they would be,

- don't feel sorry for themselves,

- don't worry about being loved; they know we love them,

- enjoy life just like other dogs,

- have much to teach us about living joyfully.

Differently-abled senior dogs view life with a simplicity and purity of emotion that we would be wise to emulate when it comes to how we see them. If you were blind, deaf or missing an arm or leg, your animal friend wouldn't see those physical "defects" as problems in your relationship. Your dog would love and support you in every way he could regardless of your "differently-abledness." Why not do the same for him?

Corrie

Chapter 10

Please Don't Feel Sorry For Me

Feeling sorry for the dog doesn't allow the dog the freedom to be happy about today. Your pity contaminates what's possible.

Marvin

This chapter is a kind of extension of the previous chapter with two more examples. Those of us who live with senior dogs that have what most people would perceive as limitations, disabilities, age-related illnesses and disease, often have a difficult time deciding whether to sing the "Poor Baby" song or act as a cheerleader, encouraging the dog to be the best version of himself that he can be right now at this time in his life.

If you've adopted or are fostering a rescue senior dog it's hard not to fall into the "poor baby" trap because you know your dog has either experienced grief, abandonment, neglect, abuse, or all of the above and has ended up as a throw-away shelter dog that hasn't been cared for physically, mentally or emotionally. Or, you may have a dog that came from a family who loved him, but he's been suddenly become homeless because of circumstances beyond his control.

Here's what's important to remember: Dogs live in the moment, and you need to be in the moment with your dog too. We have no control over what went on in the dog's past, so treating him like an invalid or a wounded warrior serves no useful purpose. Feeling sorry for the dog doesn't allow the dog the freedom to be happy about today. Your pity contaminates what's possible. Celebrate your dog's spirit, and help him live his life happily and productively. Once a dog feels safe and loved his ability to cope with his limitations is impressive—especially if he has someone he trusts acting as cheerleader.

As I'm writing this I'm thinking about dogs I've known and loved that have been and are wonderful examples of dogs that learned how to be the best versions of themselves because they had cheerleaders, not people who felt sorry for them:

Corrie was brought to a shelter by animal control because she was found wandering the streets of a big city. In terms of physical condition, Corrie was a train wreck: her skin—covered in hot spots—was greasy, dirty and matted. She had bad hips. Her teeth were awful. She hadn't been spayed, and as a result she had mammary tumors that were malignant and had metastized. Surgery to remove the tumors was performed by the shelter veterinarian, but the prognosis wasn't good so the shelter contacted Old Dog Haven and asked us to take Corrie into care as a hospice case because it was thought by the vet that she probably wouldn't live more than a couple of months.

When I went to the shelter to bring Corrie home I expected to meet an old, frail, sick dog that was withdrawn and clearly not well. Instead I was greeted by a smiling dog that jumped into my arms and said, "Let's go home."

Once home, Corrie ran into the house, greeted the other dogs, got a drink and was ready for dinner. She needed help getting up on the bed later to watch television, (Did I mention that she was a Corgi? Very short legs.) but that first day and night was the epitome of how Corrie lived life.

Corrie loved walks on the beach and became known among the regulars who walked at the same time we did as the "Official Greeter." Seeing her run on the beach to greet people is one of my favorite memories of her. Riding in the truck was always a favorite activity too—especially if a stop at Starbucks was on the itinerary.

As the days stretched into weeks and months, Corrie still smiled. She never allowed her physical issues to define who she was as a dog. Her skin cleared up, a dental helped her mouth, medication helped her arthritis, and for a while, she walked and even ran until her hips started to really bother her and she couldn't walk at all. A cart wasn't an option because her front legs were weak too. When Corrie first came to us I told her that she needed to let us know when it was time for her to move on, and one day she walked a few steps, stopped, turned around and sat down. Enough. We sent her on to her next expression of spirit the next day with love and thanks for the lessons she so graciously taught us.

For about a year and a half Corrie graced our lives with her presence. She was wise, compassionate, and playful. She was a free spirit that gave new meaning to the word "teacher."

I've made a list of some of the lessons Corrie taught us, and when you read through the list you might think that some of these lessons are only relevant if you're a dog, but I encourage you to think outside the box a bit and receive them gratefully from a gracious canine and apply them to your life as a human. You'll see what I mean:

1) When another dog barks at you and you know he isn't playing or trying to tell you that your hair is on fire, just smile and walk away.

2) Live in the moment. That's all there is.

3) Don't allow your physical difficulties to define who you are as a person.

4) Be kind and helpful.

5) Don't complain or be negative.

6) Whenever you see a ball, chase it. There might be a treat inside.

7) Stop searching for the meaning of life. It's not lost.

8) Walk your path with joy, and don't step on the flowers.

9) The glass is always half full.

10) Share your toys. It's not always about you.

11) It's all about love.

Thank you Corrie Lynn.

And then there was Marvelous Marvin. Marvin's foster mom never ceased to be amazed by her blind dog. He took long walks and galloped part of the route, he liked to wrestle with his people; they kissed his face, and he rolled all over, batting at their faces until they kissed him again. He loved to be outside, exploring or laying on a blanket in the sun, and he barked loudly at anyone coming or going, A blind guard dog! Marvin loved his weekly baths and was a great sport about all the silly costumes he wore, and having his Mohawk dyed special colors.

Marvin's foster mom said, "Marvin was ah-mazing. He was so patient; if I got frustrated for him with certain challenges, he just shrugged it off and tried again. I once told some children who felt sorry for Marvin to "feel proud of Marvin! Marvin doesn't feel sorry for himself. Marvin is proud of all he can do without being able to see."

If your dog's issue is mobility rather than visibility or hearing you may have a stroller you use when you go for walks. That's great, but you might want to let the dog walk a bit too so his sense of independence isn't compromised by always being in the stroller. Or, if your dog is too big for a stroller, try very short walks or water therapy just to help him feel that he's moving forward with his life (metaphorically and physically).

Food is another area where you may tend to fall into the "poor baby" trap. Over-feeding your dog because you feel sorry for him isn't a good idea. I know this is hard because we relate food to comfort, and if you have a dog that was very thin when he came to you, it's easy to just keep feeding large or many portions even when the dog has returned to normal weight. Carrying extra weight is hard on the heart and back. Try more hugs instead of treats.

Or perhaps the vet has diagnosed your dog with cancer that can't be treated or some other life-threatening disease, and you were told that your dog probably has only months to live. Now what?

Your dog doesn't allow disease to define who he is. He doesn't want or need pity; he just wants to be loved and cared for in the best way you can right now. It's very important in these cases that you don't grieve for your dog before he's gone; to waste precious time together by constantly thinking about the future or the past. Counting the days until the end of your dog's life is not a helpful way to view the situation. Be in the moment with your dog. Celebrate now.

I could give you dozens of other examples of dogs that are thriving because their people don't feel sorry for them, and are interested in helping the dog use whatever abilities he has to function and be happy, but I'm sure you get my point. Please understand too that I'm not suggesting that sympathy and compassion aren't appropriate emotions to express to your dog because it's also important that he understands that you know what he's experienced in his past, and what's going on with him now, but there's a big difference between positive compassion and pity.

Dogs want to be valued as they are and with a little encouragement they'll rise to the occasion and do just fine, regardless of their apparent limitations, IF you eliminate the "Poor Baby" song from your repertoire and sing "I Can Do That" as a duet with your dog. Then, as an encore you could both channel your inner Louie Armstrong and sing "What a Wonderful World."

Matt and Lucy

Chapter 11

Why Do Dogs Love People

. . . And, more to the point, they love us because they know we need the kind of love they can offer us.

Science tells us that the hormone oxytocin (more commonly called the "love hormone") is released in both dogs and people when they have a positive interaction; it cements and increases the bond.

Also, research has shown that just the smell of a person they like will make a dog happy. When a dog smells his person that smell activates a reward center in the brain called the caudate nucleus. Apparently dogs don't react the same way to any other scent.

But I think there's more to it than what I've described in the above paragraphs. I wouldn't dismiss what science tells us, but I think dogs (especially senior dogs) function intuitively and process everything emotionally so they can offer us a non-judgmental, no strings attached kind of love. And, more to the point, they love us because they know we need the kind of love they can offer us.

Human to human love is wonderful and fulfills a significant need; being loved by other people—regardless of the kind of love you're thinking about—helps center us and provides a connection to the human world that's important, but love is often conditional, and it's rarely a right now in the present non-judgmental emotional experience.

How is it possible that dogs know what we need? They know because they feel what we need. We can mask our emotional needs with all kinds of intellectual processing, but the bottom line is that underneath all of the rhetoric, how we feel guides our actions. What we think isn't nearly as important as what we feel. Dogs get that and respond to it.

We see evidence of this emotional connection between dogs and people every day: dogs helping people grieve, dogs visiting hospitals and care facilities, dogs communicating with people who have a hard time being verbal, etc. I'm sure you have your own examples.

Let's take the experience of fostering a dog for Old Dog Haven. Most fosters I've talked with say that the dog they're fostering gives them something they need and value. Our dogs fill a need in our lives that's all about grounding, validating, laughing, crying, feeling useful, living in the moment, and whatever other need comes to your mind.

Perhaps the lesson here is that if we could speak and listen from our hearts, our communication with others might be less complicated and more complete.

Chapter 12

Receiving Gifts from Your Dog

*Receive their joyful spirit and thank them
for sharing it with you.*

Randy

Receiving graciously is a gift too. Especially if the gift is from your dog. When you receive gifts from your dog, that act of receiving opens your heart just a bit wider. I made a list of some of the gifts we receive from our senior dogs, and my hope is that you'll receive all of them graciously with thanks and without reservation.

1) Another Day Together

If you live with an older dog, each day your dog is able to stay with you is a gift. Be in the moment. Enjoy the time you have together. Don't think about the "what ifs" because that kind of thinking spoils the moment.

2) Wagging Tails

When your dog wags his tail at you the message is clear: "You're my person, and I love you." Return that tail wag with a smile and a hug. I once loved a dog that was so damaged when she came to me she didn't wag her tail for a year. On the day I received that first wag I thought I'd won the lottery. That tail wag was one of the best gifts I've ever received.

3) Gifts from Outdoors

Dogs like to share what they find, and when your dog brings you a treasure he found in the yard ... even if it's yucky ... it's important to receive that gift graciously and not come unglued because you have a dead mouse on your kitchen floor or pine cones on your bed.

4) Snuggling

When your dog curls up with you on the couch and puts his head on your lap this act of intimacy is always a gift.

5) Interrupting your Work with a Nudge and Head on your Knee

If you do any work on the computer, dogs have a way of knowing when it's time to take a break, and they aren't shy about letting you know that it's time to quit and focus on them. My dog friend Josie often came to me while I was sitting at the computer. She would put her paw on my knee and sit quietly looking at me with her favorite toy in her mouth. She didn't say anything. She just stared. But if I didn't stop what I was doing for a minute and play with her she'd drop the toy at my feet, and give one bark. Message received.

6) Resilience

Those of us who live with dogs that are old and don't always feel well constantly receive the gift of optimism and perseverance from them. Dogs want to be well, and they work from a positive approach to get the most out of every day.

7) Finding Joy When You Least Expect it

Dogs know how to experience a sense of joy and to show their joyfulness in everything they do. Whether it's a ride in the car, a walk in the park, a special treat, or just being with you, they get the most out of every moment. It's that being in the moment thing they do so well. Receive their joyful spirit and thank them for sharing it with you.

8) Unconditional Love

This is a phrase that has almost become a cliché, and I find that it's most commonly used in connection with the relationship between a dog and a human. As humans, we do know how to love, but the feeling often becomes complicated and there are often expectations. No so with the unconditional love received from a dog. No strings. No hidden agendas. No conditions. No expectations. Your dog accepts you completely as you are and he loves you without reservation.

Chapter 13

Taking Photographs of Your Senior Dog

"Get down on their level! Move around and photograph from different angles."

Julie

I thought you might like a few tips from a pro about taking photographs of your senior dog, and now seems like a good time to throw the topic out for your consideration.

If you're like me, you like to take pictures of your dog, but often the results are out of focus, the head is cut-off, or you miss the "Kodak moment" and are left with less than desirable results.

So, I asked award-winning photographer, Julie Austin, to give you some tips that might be useful. Julie has been a good friend to Old Dog Haven for many years, and has taken hundreds of photographs of our dogs. Not only does Julie photograph ODH dogs, but she also photographs dogs from other rescues, as well as private clients as well. Also, Julie's photographs can often be seen on the cover of City Dog magazine, and her extraordinary photograph of ODH dog Solomon graces the cover of the book about Old Dog Haven: *Old Dog Haven: Every Old Dog Has a Story to Tell*, and yes, Julie took the photograph of Pearl, the cover dog for this book. Julie has been voted Evening Magazine's "The Best of Western Washington" Best Pet Photographer for many years. Many of Julie's photographs can be found within this book. As you can see, she has an amazing eye, and I'm so happy to have her share her work with us as well as her tips for taking photographs.

Here's what Julie Austin has to say:

- "If you are struggling to get a photograph of your deaf and/or blind dog looking at the camera, it can help to use treats. I like to give the dog a few treats first, so that they know that there is food nearby. I recommend bringing a variety in case your pet is feeling picky. My favorite treat to use is Zuke's Peanut Butter treats; they are small (so they can have as many as they want!), gluten free, and corn free. I also use squeaky toys a lot to get the dog's attention. Obviously, if your dog is hard of hearing or deaf, this may not be the route for you.

- "Get down on their level! Move around and photograph from different angles. You can also put the dog on a chair or couch to get them at eye level...as long as you don't think they will jump off! Safety first.

- "Avoid using a flash. That can turn a dog's eyes red (or green if they have cataracts). Natural light, preferably outdoors, is best.

- "Some folks think you need sunshine for photos. It's fine as long as it's not too bright (think a summer day at noon) but I prefer cloudy days. Thank goodness we have plenty of those here in the Pacific Northwest!

- "Get into the picture! Have someone take over the camera to get photos of you and your pup. Even if you hate to have your picture taken, you'll treasure the image of you with your beloved dog.

- "Take LOTS of pictures. For my typical three hour session I will take around 1,000 pictures, and approximately 50 of those are keepers. Of course, you don't need to take that many!

- "Do you have a black dog? They are notoriously challenging to photograph. I suggest to keep them out of the sun. Photograph them in a shaded area, or on a cloudy day.

- "Your dog doesn't always need to be in the center of the picture. It can be more interesting if the dog is off to the side.

- "I always suggest taking a painting or drawing class. Composition is a huge part of photography. But don't worry if you don't feel up to doing that!

- "Editing is part of my creative process. You can find inexpensive (or free) editing programs for your laptop and smart phone.

- "Take your time. Patience is key when photographing animals.

- "Have fun! If you feel like you're getting frustrated, put the camera down and just spend some time snuggling with your pooch. We all know how easily they pick up on our moods."

Thank you Julie!

Chapter 14

Disaster Preparedness for your Pets
by Julia N. Allen, Ph.D., DVM

. . . " we need to plan ahead to protect our family and care for these dogs with a disaster plan that will sustain all family members for a minimum of 30 days."

Christian with Kizzy and Albert

As I sit here in the comfort of my home, images of people carrying their dogs and cats across the border in Ukraine flash before my eyes. I see an older woman struggling to walk with a large dog draped over her shoulders, and young children pulling dogs and cats in wagons and carts. Photographs from the U.S. show families, homes and lives—including family pets—destroyed or disrupted by natural disasters.

Preparing for a disaster requires information, so I asked one of Old Dog Haven's foster moms to share what she's learned about disaster preparedness for our pets. Meet Julia N. Allen, Ph.D., DVM. Thank you, Julia.

In the event of a natural or man-made disaster, you and your pets may be forced to evacuate your home. If you and your family need to stay in a public shelter, your pets may not be permitted with you. Planning ahead for their care will help keep your mind at ease, and ensure their safety and comfort.

Even if you do not need to evacuate your home, many disasters isolate homes, neighborhoods, or communities. Again, planning ahead and having adequate supplies on hand will protect your family and your pets.

Disasters can strike quickly and without warning. Some end quickly, but others may require a long-term recovery process,which may give rise to special needs for housing and care for your pets.

First, prepare for yourself and your family by creating a family disaster plan. Knowing what to do is your best protection and your responsibility. Remember you cannot care for your pets if you are injured or unable to care for yourself.

Everyone should have at least 30 days (NOT JUST 3 DAYS) worth of food, treats, medications, water, etc. for their pets (and themselves.)

CRATE: Every dog should have a suitable crate (can be kept collapsed so as not to take up too much storage space) in case one has to stay in a hotel or in a public space of some kind. Take the time to familiarize your dog with the crate so that going in, and staying in, does not become a battle. Be sure you have absorbent bedding (e.g. towels) for each crate, and a tarp or plastic of some kind (e.g. a large garbage bag cut open) to cover it, should that be necessary. Remember you may not have heat, so making the crate warm and cozy with bedding and an outside covering will increase the comfort for your dog.

FOOD & FOOD BOWL: At least two bags of food (i.e. a 60-day supply) should always be in your house for each pet. When one bag goes empty, you start the next bag and immediately buy a replacement.

WATER & WATER BOWL: For water, consider stocking water purification tablets (for yourself and the dogs) along with your bottled water. These are easier to store and have longer dating than cases of bottled water. You can also use them to purify bottled water that has expired. There are lots of types on the market, and the fine print is important. Look for ones that are EPA approved, and that kill everything: bacteria, viruses, giardia, AND cryptosporidium. A good brand I have found is Micropur Tablets made by Katadyn, which is available on Amazon.com as well as other on-line stores.

Also consider purchasing a water filtration system (also sold on-line and in camping and backpacking stores.) They come in essentially three types – a hand pump, Ultraviolet Light, or a gravity-flow system. Many are very reasonably priced, or you can buy the Cadillac version that can filter water as contaminated as cow-pasture puddles.

With the tablets and/or a filtration system, you can drink water from local streams, ponds, etc. NOTE: These water filters and tablets do not remove chemical, petroleum, etc. contamination—only bacteria, viruses, and protozoan parasites.

MEDICATIONS: Think of them like toilet paper—get more well before you get to the end of the roll. Talk to your vet (and your doctor) about maintaining a 30-day supply, and what to do if you do run out (e.g. what to use if you run out of dry-eye drops – will OTC lubricating eye drops get you through in a crisis?)

CLEANING SUPPLIES: Think of all the things you use to keep all parts of your pets clean:

- Pooper-scooper bags, pee pads

- Tissues, moist wipes, cotton balls, paper towels

- Cloth towels

- "Wet Wipes" for when you cannot wash stuff off your hands

- A bucket or bag to collect all the waste and trash (Neat and tidy = better sanitation overall)

VACCINATIONS & ID: Many pets will get loose and become lost during a disaster. Be sure your dog always wears a properly fitted collar or harness, and keep the rabies tag on your dog's collar along with the tag with your address and phone. All pets should be microchipped without exception, and that microchip should be registered to the owner (not the Shelter or Vet Hospital.) Be sure YOU have the microchip number written down. Make a copy of your Rabies Vaccination Certificate, and keep it in a plastic sleeve with your crate.

PHOTOS: If your dog escapes and becomes lost, you will want to post a photo at your local Community Disaster Center, and also on-line. Therefore, keep pictures of your pets on your phone, and print several copies off your computer for each dog (black and white is fine.) Write their name, microchip number, and your name/address/number on each photo, and then put them individually in a plastic sleeve with your crate.

CLOTHES AND BLANKETS AND BEDS: Remember things may get wet and you may not be able to dry them like you usually do. You may not have heat of any kind. Wet harnesses and nylon collars that remain on your dog for a period of time could cause a skin infection. Dry dog-coats and bedding are essential to keeping your dog warm. Those industrial strength X-large "contractor cleanup bags" can be repurposed for a myriad of uses. Buy a big box.

AWAY FROM HOME: Consider what you would do if you are away from home without your pets when disaster strikes, and what will happen if you cannot get home in a timely fashion. Do you have a neighbor that loves dogs with a key to your house who could go over and care for your pets until you are able to get home? Also what do you do if you are driving somewhere with your pets in the car and you become stranded? The emergency kit in your car should include at least some food and water and for all of you, towels, and few of those heavy duty black plastic bags.

AT THE TIME OF THE DISASTER: For an earthquake: drop, cover, and hold is still step one. Then at your first opportunity put your dog in the crate. With a disaster threatening your home and family, your pet will sense the stress and may run away in panic or hide. The crate will provide the dog with containment in a safe place while you assess the situation. By securing your dog promptly, you can concentrate on caring for yourself, your family, AND your dog.

Listen to the Emergency Broadcast System for information and instructions. Take note of any specific instructions for companion animals.

If you leave your home with your dog, make sure you have all the supplies you have prepared. Once at your destination, remember your normally loving dog will be very frightened. This fear may cause him to run away or become aggressive even toward you. Keep your dog in the crate with the door closed, and reassure him. Remove him from the crate only when he is calm, and on a leash in a closed space where he cannot escape.

AFTER THE DISASTER: Use caution in allowing any pet outdoors after the disaster has passed. Familiar scents and landmarks may be altered and your dog could easily be confused even on his own property. Downed power lines, stray animals, broken glass, etc. present real dangers for your dog.

If your dog is lost during the disaster, contact veterinary hospitals, animal control facilities, and any emergency sheltering facilities that may have been set up by rescue groups. You should go to these shelters in person and look for your dog, and search the photos in on-line data bases, rather than rely on phone descriptions.

If you find a pet, contact any phone numbers that may have been set up during the disaster to report lost and found animals. If the pet is injured, contact your veterinarian or any emergency care facility that may have also been set up.

IN SUMMARY: Experience with disasters throughout the country has taught us many valuable lessons. However, pets are still not allowed in Red Cross emergency shelters, and commonly pets are still not prepared for adequately at the local level. Food and water are transported in for people, but not for animals. In large disasters, communities have primarily relied on the national non-profit animal rescue groups like HSUS or the ASPCA, and thankfully they have become well organized and very efficient at providing emergency animal sheltering services especially for stray and unattended animals.

But for OLD dogs, with their often complex medical issues, abandonment, and previous public shelter experience, these types of disaster shelters are a very poor option. Instead, we need to plan ahead to protect our family and care for these dogs with a disaster plan that will sustain all family members for a minimum of 30 days.

Our dogs are depending on us to be well prepared.

Moon

Chapter 15

Incontinence

I think basically there are three main reasons for incontinence in senior dogs.

Jenny ended up in a shelter because she was peeing in the house. Apparently she'd been incontinent for quite a while, but Jenny was never brought to a vet to determine the cause of the problem. Most shelters don't have the financial resources to pay for extensive vet exams or surgery, so Old Dog Haven was asked to intervene, and Jenny was immediately examined by one of our vets. Two bladder stones (one quite large) were discovered. The bladder stones were causing bloody urine and a significant degree of discomfort for Jenny. Thanks to Old Dog Haven, Jenny immediately received the surgery she needed to remove the bladder stones and is recovering nicely in one of our foster homes ... no longer incontinent.

Like Jenny, many senior dogs find themselves in shelters because of incontinence. Sometimes the person surrendering the dog is honest about the issue, but more often than not the shelter isn't told, and once the dog is an actual shelter resident determining incontinence is difficult because dog behavior often changes quite drastically in a shelter.

I mention Jenny because I'd like to offer a few thoughts about the issue of incontinence in a home situation. Does your senior dog pee in the house? There are many articles available online that give detailed information that you might find helpful, but I think basically there are three main reasons for incontinence in senior dogs:

1) Physical Issues

Perhaps something is going on in your dog's body that is causing the incontinence. Arthritis in the spine? Neurological issues? Hormonal imbalance? Urinary infections? Bladder stones? Kidney disease? Diabetes? You need to have a vet examine your dog to determine the cause of the incontinence. Should your vet rule out any underlying disease or illness as being the cause of your dog's incontinence, he or she may decide to put your dog on medication. Many incontinence drugs that are given will help improve the tone of the muscles that hold urine in the bladder. Your vet will tell you which of these are most appropriate for your dog.

2) Emotional Issues

Stress is an often over-looked cause of incontinence because it isn't a physical problem, but it certainly shouldn't be ruled out in terms of a factor contributing to incontinence. Dogs process everything emotionally, and if they feel stressed, their bodies can't help but react to how they feel. Here you need to ask yourself what's going on in your home that would be causing your dog to feel stressed. Are you spending less time with your dog? Has there been a change in family dynamics? How about a recent move? Or, perhaps there's a new baby in the house? Have you been ill and your dog is worried about you? Is there a new dog in the house? You get the idea. Once you figure out the cause of your dog's stress, you'll have a better idea about how to deal with the issue.

3) Mental Issues

It's not unusual for a dog suffering from dementia to become incontinent. Confusion, impaired thinking, and general lack of awareness contribute to a dog's inability to control his bodily functions.

I could talk in depth about each one of the reasons I've mentioned, but all I want to do here is to ask you to address the issue as it might apply to you.

First and most importantly, please take your dog to the vet to find out whether the cause is physical. If your vet finds a physical reason for the incontinence, a course of treatment will be prescribed, and hopefully you will see good results.

If the cause is emotional, your job here will be to determine what's causing the stress contributing to the incontinence and work to eliminate the stress.

If you're dealing with dementia, the problem of incontinence is liable to be chronic and perhaps not treatable, so you might want to look at the various products (pee pads, diapers, belly bands, etc.) available to help with the problem. Talk to other people to see what has worked for them.

Martha Anne

Chapter 16

You Don't Own Me

For me, regardless of what the law says, people who see themselves as owners of their dog (or any other animal) are missing the point of living with a dog.

Even though some states are dancing around the issue, dogs (and other animals) are considered property or possessions in the eyes of the law. Along with that designation comes the generally accepted mentality that people are owners of their animals. As possessions, dogs are bred for money, raised in puppy mills for monetary gain, sold in pet stories, forced to be a part of the racing circuit (now thankfully illegal in most states), entered in shows, used for entertainment, and exploited in many other ways.

While it is true that in the U.S. there are certain laws designed to protect animals from abuse and neglect, those laws are often very difficult to enforce and are generally not strong enough to really protect animals at risk. That's a whole different topic of discussion.

So, what's the real issue here? For me, regardless of what the law says, people who see themselves as owners of their dog (or any other animal) are missing the point of living with a dog. To place a monetary value on your dog suggests that your dog is very much like your toaster or your car. You own the inanimate objects in your life, but to put your dog in the same category as your couch or television dismisses the value of a living being in your home. To think that you own your dog is showing a lack of respect and value for the presence of the dog in your life. And no, I'm not saying that dogs are like people and should be treated as such. Dogs are dogs, and humanizing them not only does them a disservice, but completely ignores their value as a life form.

I'm guessing that most of you reading this book don't think of your dogs as property, but I'll bet many of you do use the word "owner" to describe your relationship to your dog. Maybe you don't mean to imply that your dog is just a possession, but words can take on lives of their own when they're used often enough.

What we think, feel and do creates an energy that generates a ripple effect. (More about this later.) The words we use do the same thing. If what I'm saying here resonates with you in some way, the next time you hear yourself using the word "owner" to describe your relationship with your dog, stop and use a word that more closely fits what you feel your relationship really is to your companion—i.e. friend, guardian, or caregiver. Then, pay it forward. If you hear someone use the word "owner" to describe their relationship to their dog ask them to really think about what they're saying.

I wonder how long it will take the U.S. to catch up to France where, according to law, animals are considered to be "living and feeling beings."

Chapter 17

Love a Dog, Live Longer

It's an intangible and yet powerful connection that helps you live your life positively and productively.

Gary and Oliver

Scientists, medical personnel, psychologists and pretty much every kind of people/animal professional all seem to agree that many people who share their lives with dogs live longer than people who don't share their homes and hearts with dogs.

For those of you who live with dogs (and that's probably almost everyone reading this book) the above paragraph is a no-brainer and you're probably thinking, "Why is she telling me this? I already know it's true." "I get more exercise because I walk with my dog." "My dog helps me lower my blood pressure and relieve stress." "My heart is healthier." "So what's the big deal?"

The big deal is the why. Why do people who love and live with dogs tend to live longer? Yeah, I know about the exercise, stress reducing benefits, responsibility factor, etc. but that information doesn't answer the question. Those are just body/mind benefits. What is it about dogs that helps people live longer and healthier lives?

Here's my answer: Dogs process everything emotionally, unlike people who tend to complicate things by analyzing and intellectualizing. When you connect with a dog on an emotional level that's a straight-line connection unlike any other you could experience. That connection provides a positive effect on your life IF you allow it to do so because the connection is so strong it erases the negative. Some people call this connection unconditional love, but it's more than that. It's everything good and life-affirming. It's an intangible and yet powerful connection that helps you live your life positively and productively. It's a connection that's difficult to make with another human being because there's too much other stuff in the way.

I'm smiling as I write this because here I am talking to you about why connecting with a dog on an emotional level can help you live longer and yet I'm using words. One of the frustrating fringe benefits of being human I guess—needing words to communicate.

Forget about the words. Let your love for your dog guide you to a longer, happier life.

Emi

Chapter 18

Separation Anxiety

. . . two things that might be at work here: loss and change.

Does your dog suffer from separation anxiety? If so, perhaps I can offer a few thoughts that might be of some help. This will be a kind of "Reader's Digest" discussion, but if you need more information there's an excellent article by the ASP-CA on the Internet that offers more detailed information.

Ok, so let's talk about symptoms you might see if you think your dog is dealing with separation anxiety:

- Peeing and/or pooping in the house
- Barking, whining, howling
- Loss of appetite
- Destructive behavior
- Drooling
- Escaping from the house or yard
- Chewing
- Digging
- Pacing
- Depression

If you're seeing any of these behaviors, as always, I recommend that you check with your vet to rule out any physical cause, but once you do that, you need to understand the why behind the behavior.

There doesn't seem to be any conclusive evidence related to the question of why some dogs suffer from separation anxiety, but I've narrowed the possibilities down to two things that might be at work here: loss and change.

Dogs, like many people, feel safe and comfortable if there's a routine in place that they can depend on every day. If that routine is disrupted, temporarily or permanently, the dog may feel insecure and anxious. Dogs coming from shelters suffer from separation anxiety more than dogs that have lived in one home for their whole lives because when they end up in a shelter, there's definitely a change in routine that comes with a loss of home and family. Life has changed dramatically for them, especially if they've ended up in the shelter because their person has died and they've lived in only one home their whole life. Adjusting to a new home may be difficult and cause them to become anxious.

So, you need to ask yourself what changes have occurred recently in your dog's life? What loss has he experienced? Have the family dynamics changed? Has there been a divorce? Has someone within the family died? Have you moved recently? Has another dog in the family died recently? Are you ill and is your dog worried about you? I could go one, but you understand what I'm saying here.

Remember that dogs process everything emotionally so adjusting to change and loss is hard for them sometimes. Here's where you come into the picture. Patience. Patience.

And more patience. There's no quick fix here. Helping a dog deal with separation anxiety is often a long process requiring you to take baby steps and be patient. Try these things:

- Lots of physical contact with your dog

- Leave the house for only short periods of time at first. (I'm talking minutes here.) Try putting your dog in the bedroom, shutting the door and walking away for a few minutes before you graduate to the front door.

- When you leave, tell your dog you'll be back. (Yes, he'll understand you.)

- Leave music playing—not hard rock, but soothing, soft music.

- If you have other dogs make sure they're all together in the same room if you have to go somewhere and can't take them with you.

- Offer calming treats before you go and when you come home.

- Calming pet beds

- Weighted blankets

- Thundershirts

- Laundry basket full of dirty clothes that smell like you.

Finally, think about what you need to deal with loss and change. What would you do or have you done to help yourself, and then translate those things to helping your dog.

Chapter 19

Is Your Senior Dog Overweight?

Talk to your vet to come up with a weight loss plan for your dog.

Tigger

Did you know that about 53% of senior dogs are overweight, and more than 22% of dog caregivers don't realize that their senior dog is carrying too much weight? Let's talk about this disturbing bit of information.

First, let me talk a bit about the emotional component here: If your senior dog is a rescue and/or has had a difficult past, it's hard to not overfeed him because you're trying to make up for a background which may have involved not eating enough or not being loved enough. Food is a great pacifier—for both humans and animals—and rewarding through food is very common. Somehow for many, nothing says "I love you" better than lots of treats, whether we're talking about a dog or a person.

So, how can you tell if your dog is obese? You should be able to easily feel your dog's ribs when you place your hands on his ribcage, and there should be a waist that is easily seen. Try it. Right now. Well?

The medical impacts of obesity are serious, and when a dog is in his senior years the effect is compounded. Possible health risks include:

- **Surgical risk:** Senior dogs are already a high risk group when it comes to surgery, but when weight is an issue, the risks are even greater. Increased fat in the tissues makes surgery itself more difficult. Surgery on an overweight dog is more technically difficult, and the procedure takes longer than usual, which again increases the anesthesia risk.

- **Respiratory Decline:** Overweight dogs carry excess fat and this can often restrict the lungs' ability to expand making breathing difficult. By stressing the body and its key organs most dogs lose a great deal of stamina and endurance.

- **Heart disease and increased blood pressure:** As the body is being asked to work harder, overweight and obese dogs are at risk of heart complications. Dogs can suffer from hypertension too, and carrying around extra weight contributes to the problem. High blood pressure can lead to congestive heart failure.

- **Damage to joints, bones and ligaments:** Carrying around the extra weight can lead to joint complications and dogs can develop arthritis. If your dog already has arthritis or other joint problems then the pain and discomfort can become increasingly worse due to the extra weight load.

What can you do to help your senior dog lose weight? Despite the challenges that senior dogs face, there are ways to control their weight and keep them active. The consequences of not addressing weight issues are too serious to ignore. Your dog isn't feeding himself; controlling your dog's weight is your responsibility as his caregiver. Try these things:

- **Talk to your vet** to come up with a weight loss plan for your dog. Figure out how much weight your dog needs to lose and then look at how to achieve that goal.

- **Switching to a lower calorie food** may make sense or simply feeding a bit less of your dog's current diet may work. Look for the food that says "low fat."

- **Reduce the number of treats** or switch to healthier, lower calorie treats. Many dogs love pieces of apple, carrot or green beans. If your dog is used to getting two treats at bedtime, break one treat into two pieces. Yes, I know dogs can count, but you can always use the "it's for your own good" line.

- **Swimming or walking in water** not only helps get rid of fat but is good training for muscles and is easy on the joints.

- **Exercise.** If your dog has mobility issues, exercising may be a little tricky, but a little bit of exercise each day will help with weight loss.

Losing weight takes discipline—for both dogs and humans—but in the long run the results are well worth the effort.

Thomas (black dog) and Friend

Chapter 20

So Much Joy

. . . their recognition of a shared past and a hopeful future created a bond that was tangible.

My idea of a good time is to be around dogs. Whether it's walking dogs at the shelter or spending time with my own dogs, being with dogs makes me a happy camper. I especially like spending time with senior dogs that were once homeless and are now happy and healthy because they've either been adopted or are being permanently fostered by Old Dog Haven's amazing network of foster parents. So, with those thoughts in mind let me tell you about one of my favorite good times.

You already know that I'm involved with Old Dog Haven, so with that in mind I want to tell you about a picnic Old Dog Haven hosted for fosters and other volunteers. Not everyone could come, but about 140 of our people were there with their dogs—a long trip for those who live in Portland, Vancouver, Olympia, Bellingham and Spokane.

Our people. That sense of identity was so apparent as I walked around meeting dogs and visiting with people. As one foster mom put it, "It's so nice to be among my people. Great food, conversation, goodies for the pups. A truly blissful day."

That sense of belonging was evident as I interacted with the dogs too; they knew they were with their extended family. Even dogs that were blind, deaf or both were comfortable in the large group of people and other dogs. This was especially true in the case of my friend Rufus—a dog I first met when he was at the shelter where I walk dogs. Rufus, described by his foster mom as "the love of my doggy life," was perfectly comfortable milling around the crowd even though he was deaf and blind. I loved seeing him so happy and secure.

In addition to the love being shared by both people and dogs there was a swap tent where everyone found all kinds of goodies for their dogs. People brought what they couldn't use and shared with others. I also saw many items that could only have been donated by pet stores; thank you to them for their generosity. I think the dogs enjoyed rooting through the toys best of all and I saw several dogs walk away with toys they thought would be perfect for them, and one guy had three toys stuffed in his mouth; if he could have smiled without dropping the toys he would have done that. It was kind of like a visit to a pet store only everything was free.

That's another thing I felt at the picnic. The dogs felt free to be who they are. No more shelter stress. No more pain from whatever was troubling them. No more wondering if someone would ever love them and provide a home for them. There were other dogs there that I'd first met at the shelter, and I could see—months later—that they now know who they are and are loving that sense of identity and belonging.

And the stories I heard: To listen to the pride in the voice of a foster parent as he talked about how proud he was of his dog. To hear someone say, "You should have seen her when she first came to me. She hardly had any hair, her teeth were awful and she just hid under the bed." (This comment about a dog that was giving new meaning to the term "social butterfly" at the picnic.) To talk with a transport volunteer who'd just seen the dog she'd transported from the shelter to her foster home several months ago. She could hardly believe it was the same dog. It's all about transformation.

You know what else was really wonderful? As I watched dogs checking each other out I could sense that they all felt like kindred spirits. They knew that they'd all come from similar situations, and their recognition of a shared past and a hopeful future created a bond that was tangible. At one point I saw two dogs staring at each other. Their respective people just stood and watched because somehow they knew that this was a "moment." The dogs didn't know each other (at least not in this life) but they studied each other and then, as if on cue, both moved forward and touched noses.

What I saw and heard as I walked around hugging dogs and people was like a chorus of *Halleluiah* sung in many different languages. Many voices—both dog and human—blended together to make the most beautiful music: a woman laughing as her dog rooted around in the swap meet items looking for just the right toy, a dog snoring because he was tired of socializing and needed a nap, a man whispering to the small dog he held in his arms, a bouncy dog yipping because he wanted to share his friend's lunch, a big dog barking just because he couldn't decide which dog to chase, and a group of people cheering because the dog they were admiring howled a bit in happiness just for them.

At one point I leaned against a tree and just listened with my eyes closed. Even without seeing the smiles and hugs, I could hear the symphony of contentment that permeated the atmosphere of the day. So much joy. So much love. Halleluiah indeed.

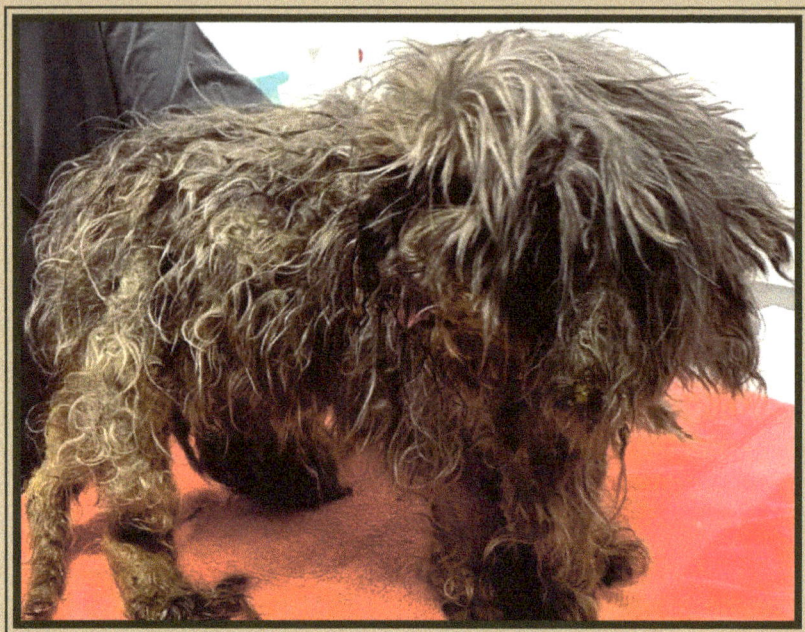

Ruthie before rescue

Ruthie after

Chapter 21

Becoming Part of the Ripple Effect

What one individual or organization does makes a difference, and that difference becomes more than just a single act because the positive energy generated spreads like a ripple effect.

We don't live in a vacuum. What we think, feel and do creates an energy that generates a ripple effect, just like a pebble dropped in the water. If that energy and the actions that go along with it are positive, the ripple effect generated will make a positive difference.

Even though shelters are filled with dogs that have been abused, neglected or abandoned, volunteers who spend time with the dogs create a ripple effect by just being there: the dogs are able to exercise and play, other people become interested in volunteering when volunteers talk about their experiences, the past becomes a dim memory for dogs that have been through terrible experiences because volunteers and staff are committed to replacing fear with love, dogs find themselves in the company of people who care about them, people read about dogs posted on the shelter website, and they make a donation to the shelter or perhaps adopt a dog.

Look on the internet for images of people helping dogs. You'll see photos of everything from a truck driver stopping traffic so he could pick up a dog on the road, to a man saving a drowning dog. People see these photos, read the stories, think positive thoughts about the dogs and people involved, and are inspired to pay it forward given a similar situation. People read about the dogs taken in by rescue groups, and they make a donation, decide to foster a dog, or at the very least become more aware of what can be done to help senior dogs in need, and they pass the word on to other people.

The simple act of hugging your dog sends out loving energy that creates a ripple effect.

All over the U.S. local laws and ordinances regarding chaining dogs are changing because more people are willing to give voice to their concerns.

Pet stores are beginning to partner with shelters rather than buying dogs from puppy mills, and individuals are becoming more willing to adopt from shelters and rescue groups rather than buying puppy mill dogs.

The Humane Society of the U.S. is actively working to decrease and eventually end the use of dogs (and other animals) in testing, research and teaching by promoting the development of innovative and effective alternative methods.

Dogfighting is a felony offense in all 50 states, and it is a felony offense under federal law as well.

There's still much that needs to be changed in the last four examples, but that doesn't mean we shouldn't represent dogs in need by being their voices. What one individual or organization does makes a difference, and that difference becomes more than just a single act because the positive energy generated spreads like a ripple effect.

And, it's not just about the dog. When you share your heart with a dog, something happens to you too. Because of what you feel for your dog, your interactions with others change too: Perhaps what you feel is translated into a kind of "pay it forward" attitude that inspires you to help others ... not just dogs, but people. What you learn about compassion influences your relationships with other people.

Here's an example of what I'm talking about: Mark lost both of his legs because he was injured in an accident. To say that Mark was depressed would be an understatement. His physical therapy was slow because he was too busy feeling sorry for himself to do the work needed to allow him to function in a wheelchair. He just couldn't get out of his own way.

Until ... one day someone brought a dog that also didn't have the use of his back legs and was using a cart ... to one of Mark's therapy sessions. Mark watched the dog work the room, interacting with everyone there, smiling and wagging his tail.

That day was the beginning of a relationship between Mark and Buddy the dog that created a ripple effect in Mark's life. He was inspired by Buddy's determination and began to really work hard to use his wheelchair. He started encouraging others who had the same issues, he smiled and laughed, joined a basketball team of peope who were in wheelchairs too, and in general Mark's attitude inspired others. He paid it forward. I have no idea how many people were helped by Mark, but the ripple effect was far-reaching.

**Be a part of the ripple effect. Or better yet,
be that pebble dropped in the water.**

"Just as ripples spread out when a single pebble is dropped into water, the actions of individuals have far-reaching effects."

~ *Dalai Lama*

Honey Deux

Chapter 22

May I Be of Service?

Dogs get people.

Joyce is sitting quietly on the couch. She's not looking at anything in particular. Just staring. Toby, age 13, the therapy dog for the care facility, walks over to her, sits in front of her and puts his paw on her knee. Joyce stirs, reaches down, picks him up and puts him on her lap. He settles down immediately as she starts to stroke his soft fur. Soon Joyce begins to talk to Toby. She tells him about feeding the chickens, sitting in school, the new coat she got for Christmas, what she did on her 12th birthday and how she doesn't like green beans. This monologue wouldn't be unusual except that Joyce, an Alzheimer's patient, doesn't talk with anyone. Except Toby.

In another city, children have been brought by their parents to the library where they'll have an opportunity to read to dogs. One boy, Karl, is 10 years old, and he's afraid to read out loud to people, but he will read to dogs. On this day Karl is joined by Missy, the golden retriever, age 12. Karl is sitting on the floor so Missy comes over to him and lays down next to him. Someone hands Karl a book, and he stretches out with his head on Missy's back and he starts to read to her. Both boy are dog are perfectly comfortable. This event happens once a week and Karl's parents say that because of his experiences reading to Missy, he's started to read a bit out loud at home.

George is blind, but with the help of his guide dog, Honey, (age 9) he's able to function quite well, as is Tracy, who doesn't hear well but her dog Tommy (age 8) alerts her to noises she needs to hear.

Baloo, a big, old, smelly, hound dog was removed from the shelter by Old Dog Haven and placed with a family that included two autistic children. Prior to Baloo's arrival, the kids struggled on many levels, but Baloo's presence made a huge difference in their lives. Baloo allowed Mollee to pull him all over in a wagon, and to dress him up in hats and necklaces. Keneau was in a rage most of the time, except when he climbed on Baloo's back and wrapped his arms around the big dog. Soon the rage passed and Keneau was calm.

I could go on with other examples, but I'm sure you see the pattern here. Older dogs can not only be friends and companions, but they can be of service to people in many ways. Whether we're talking about an official, registered service dog, or the family dog that sleeps with Judy to help her deal with nightmares, a senior dog can be of tremendous service to human beings.

How is that? What's going on with the dogs mentioned in the above paragraphs? What was going on with Buddy, the dog I talked about in the last chapter? How do they know what to do? Or not do?

Dogs get people. They know how to be in the moment with them, they feel their pain, they have the ability to focus on what people need and give it to them. Empathy. Support. Encouragement. Peace. A sense of wholeness. Love.

Would your senior dog like to spend time helping people? Why not ask him.

Chapter 23

Getting Involved: Be a Good Samaritan

. . . why not focus on helping the dog rather than judging the person?

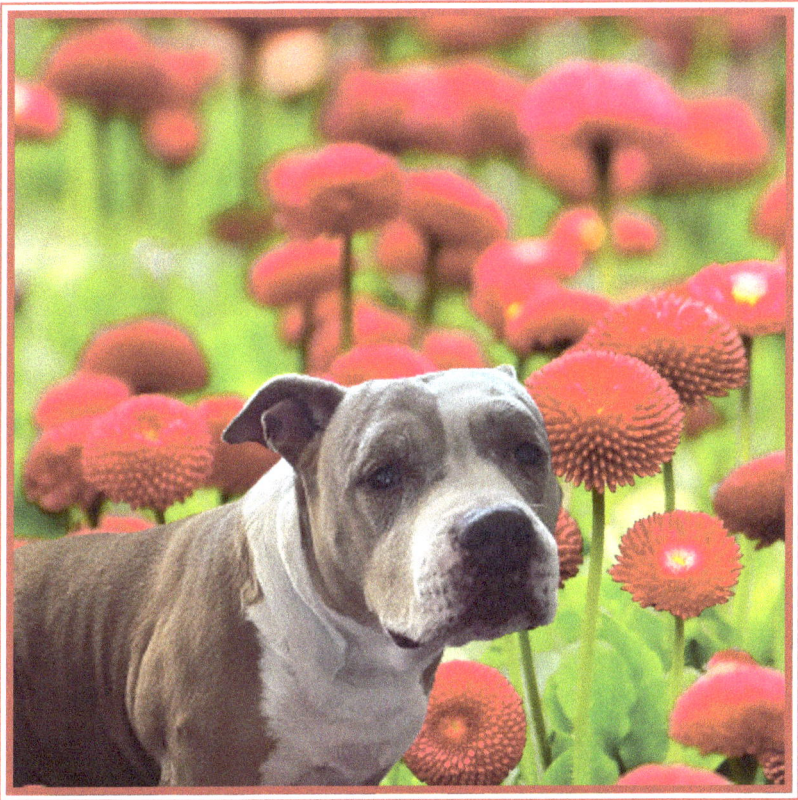

Cali

Do you have a relative, friend, or neighbor who is neglecting their dog? I'm not talking about a dog that just needs a bath or perhaps a haircut, I'm talking about a dog that has toe nails growing into his paws, skin that has been itched raw because of fleas or some kind of allergy, a coat that is matted and dirty, is either severely over or underweight, perhaps is chained outside most of the time, and in general looks like a train wreck. And that's just on the outside.

I'm asking this question because I'm hoping you're willing to help. No, I'm not asking for donations, I'm asking you to help BEFORE the dog ends up in a shelter … damaged with a broken body and broken spirit.

Old Dog Haven and other rescue groups are constantly—and I do mean constantly—being asked to take in dogs from elderly people who can no longer care for them. Or, in many cases the rescue is asked to help people with their dogs' medical care because they're struggling financially. Most of the time these dogs are in terrible physical shape from unintentional neglect; the dogs suffer because their people can't afford care for them. And, what's even more devastating is that too often people have to give up their dogs because they can't afford needed care. The dogs end up in shelters, and then—if they're fortunate—come to a rescue like Old Dog Haven with long-neglected medical issues or just "deferred maintenance" and they're miserable. And then there are the dogs that come to us suffering from neglect that can't possibly be unintentional. We do everything we can to help any neglected dog that comes to us, but sometimes the damage is so severe that the dog's quality of life is compromised beyond help, and the kindest thing we can do is to let the dog move on to his next expression of spirit.

If you know of an elderly or financially challenged friend, neighbor or family member who needs help getting vet care for their dog, you can help. How about volunteering to take the dog to the vet? Seems like that would be a wonderful gift you could offer both the dog and the person. Perhaps the vet visit could be a birthday/holiday gift for a relative? Or maybe it would be just a gesture of kindness for a neighbor or friend. Or your willingness to help might make it possible for an elderly person to still be able to keep his or her dog. If there are medications involved once the dog has seen the vet, perhaps you could ask someone else you know to step up and help with that part.

Perhaps some of you are thinking that people shouldn't have dogs if they can't afford to care for them, so why should you pay someone else's vet bills? Or why should you drive someone else's dog to the vet? After all, the dog isn't your responsibility. In theory your thinking might be accurate, but sometimes the realities of life don't hold up to theories. More importantly, why not focus on helping the dog rather than judging the person? Dogs live their lives subject to the choices people make (or don't make) about them, and if helping dogs is something you want to do, what I'm suggesting is one way to do that.

Remember what I said about the ripple effect? What I'm talking about here is a great example of how the ripple effect works. I'm thinking that if everyone reading this book could help out one person they know who loves their dog but can't afford important care, every one of you could make a huge difference in not only the life of a person but also a dog.

There's also another part of helping a dog that's being neglected that I need to mention. This is the hard part. If you have a relative, friend or neighbor who is neglecting their dog and your offers to help are rejected, please don't walk away and ignore what you see. For the sake of the dog, get involved.

The situation may fall into the "unintentional" neglect that I mentioned earlier, but more than likely the situation doesn't involve a positive relationship between the dog and his person. I'm talking about dogs that are treated like possessions rather than family members, and even as possessions they aren't maintained even nearly as well as household items.

If you know of a dog that's being neglected and your offer to do any or all of the things to help that I've mentioned in earlier paragraphs is refused, it's time to take it to the next level. Contact Animal Control and ask them to do a welfare check on the dog. Think about the welfare of the dog.

You don't want to get involved? You don't want your relative, friend or neighbor to be angry with you? If you say or do nothing you become part of the problem rather than a voice that contributes to the solution. For the sake of the dog, **please get involved!**

Chapter 24

Planning Ahead and Following Up on the Plan

Dogs suffer the consequences of the actions or lack of action of people.

Honaleigh

What will happen to your dog if you are no longer able to care for him?

Shelters are filled with dogs that ended up there because their people were unable to care for them. It's important to make plans NOW (never mind how old you are or how secure your home situation seems to be) or your precious friend could end up being passed around from one home to another, confused and lost, only to end up in a shelter where his future is uncertain ... especially if he's a senior dog.

Don't just presume that your family or friends will assume responsibility for your dog if you are no longer able to care for him. People often say they'll take care of your dog if your life changes or if you die, but I've seen far too many situations where the promise isn't kept and the dog ends up in a shelter.

Here's what I suggest you do:

- Think carefully about the needs of your dog and make a decision now about who will care for him if your life changes in a way that makes caring for your dog impossible.

- Talk to family members and friends about whether they might be ready and willing to care for your dog in case you're unable to do so.

- Be sure that the person you've chosen as your dog's future guardian is serious about taking on the responsibility of caring for your friend, and is willing to make a commitment to you.

- Talk to the person you've chosen about your animal's needs, and make sure that this person knows the name of your veterinarian. It's important that the dog's health records can be easily located.

- Give the name and phone number of the guardian to your veterinarian and to your family if this person is not a family member.

- Include information about the guardian in your will.

- Keep a notebook of all of the information about your dog's habits, needs, likes, dislikes, etc. and tell the guardian where this notebook can be found in your home.

- Keep a card in your wallet with the name, phone number and address of your guardian so he or she can be notified immediately if you are unable to make contact.

- Determine whether you'll need to provide in your will for the costs of caring for your friend.

- Socialize your dog. A dog that is well-socialized with other animals and people has a much greater chance of fitting in to a new situation where there will be new people and possibly other animals.

Finally ... and I know you don't want to hear this ... if you really can't find anyone that you're absolutely sure will be able to take your dog into his or her home, and your dog is a senior in poor health, the kindest option might be for you to consider specifying euthanasia for your dog rather than letting your friend go to a shelter. I've spent many years with shelter dogs, and I can't even begin to tell you how heartbreaking it is to watch an old, sick dog that came from a loving family try to understand why he's there. Don't ask your dog to trade emotional well-being for stress and depression. Dying by inches in a cage surrounded by strangers is no way to leave this life.

Ok, so I've talked about the planning ahead part, now let's talk about following through on the plan. It's very important to monitor whatever plan is chosen, because in some cases, as is true in the story I'm about to tell you, end of life decisions for humans may begin long before the actual end of life, and they often involve loss of control due to many forms of cognitive dysfunction. Often, as is true in this story, caregivers do not always consider the best interests of the animal involved, and the results can be devastating. In telling the story I'm not going to use real names—of the people involved or the dog—because that would serve no useful purpose and my goal here is to offer lessons to be learned.

Louise is an elderly woman who wanted to adopt a big dog from a shelter, so three years ago she went to a local shelter with Mary, her Power of Attorney. She adopted Leon—a large, healthy, active, seven year-old dog that had been at the shelter a while.

Louise suffered from dementia (already diagnosed when she adopted Leon) and eventually went to live in an assisted living/memory care facility. Leon went with her but it soon became clear to the staff that Louise was unable to care for him. The final straw was when Leon started peeing all over the facility because Louise was incapable of remembering to take him outside. As she apparently had been doing ever since she first adopted him, Louise fed Leon constantly and at one point he weighed 126.5 pounds. (A healthy weight for Leon is between 70-75 pounds.) Because Louise was unable to care for Leon, and she was told that she had to find another place for him to live, Louise then hired (through her POA, Mary) Sheila to care for Leon.

It wasn't long before Sheila's neighbors became concerned about Leon's welfare. He wasn't allowed in the house, and could be heard crying at the door. The yard wasn't fenced so he was tied up outside or left to wander the neighborhood. He frequently had no water and wasn't fed on a regular basis. Neighbors did what they could to help Leon, including talking to Sheila and calling Animal Control, but still he remained where he was. One neighbor in particular, Rose, even took Leon to the vet on one occasion, and finally was so worried about him she called Old Dog Haven to see if we would take him because he was clearly in bad shape.

It was explained to Rose that Leon needed to be surrendered by his legal owner (Yeah, I know ... there's that word, but it's required by law that the word "owner" be used by shelters and rescue groups) before we could intervene. Eventually that happened, and Leon went to live with Nancy, a very experienced foster mom.

Since he's been with Nancy, Leon has had multiple vet visits, which included blood work, x-rays and a complete physical exam. He's also seen a dermatologist and an ophthalmologist. He's being treated four times a day for all of his medical issues, is on a special diet and gets regular exercise to help him lose weight. (He now weighs 98.5 pounds.)

That's the bare bones version of the story.

This is what Leon's foster mom has to say about Leon:

"After I picked Leon up at the vet hospital where he'd been brought by Mary I came home with a giant, very obese, depressed dog that could barely walk, barely weight bearing when he did walk, could not rise on his own, could not go up any stairs, had huge skin lesions, itched all over, had swollen eyes from itching and rubbing, had draining tracts on the bottoms of his feet, and horribly inflamed ears—just for starters.

"Further vet visits show that Leon has low thyroid, severe arthritic change in his spine, and a mass in his abdomen—probably on the spleen or could be on the liver.

"Leon has been a struggle physically for me but I got a Help-'Em-Up Harness, and that has helped me lift him and get him moving. He has perked up, and is more mobile already (especially with the harness), and I think once we get his thyroid supplemented, he may be even better.

"With all his new medications and treatments, Leon is starting to improve. He's now able to get up on his own, and he goes out for an actual walk three times per day. He started at only being able to stand and move for ten minutes at a time, but now he's up to 20-30 minutes. His skin is improving, the itching has become less, but is not resolved. Everything is a work in progress, and there is a very long road ahead.

"But the best thing is that he is no longer depressed. He wags his tail, smiles, tries to jump up in his excitement to go out for walkies, and loves to lay on the front porch with his Old Dog Haven family and watch the world go by. Leon has learned that this is his forever home, and now when he's loaded in the car for yet another trip to the vet, he knows this is where he will come back to. If it were not for Old Dog Haven, Leon would still be somewhere in limbo suffering with his pain. This is a dog that REALLY needed someone to intervene for his final days."

Ok, so now I'd like you to consider the lessons available to be learned from Leon's story:

1) As I said earlier, planning ahead in the event that you're unable to care for your dog is very important. But, any kind of plan needs monitoring, especially if there are cognitive issues involved, and there needs to be an active support system in place.

2) Shelters need to carefully screen adoptions to senior citizens. In theory, adopting a senior dog to a senior human is a wonderful idea, and is very often successful on many

levels, but when an elderly person is mentally and legally unable to make decisions for herself, that should be a red flag.

3) People who serve as a POA for an elderly person with dementia (or anyone for that matter) really need to stay on top of the situation, especially if there's an animal involved that needs care, medical attention and exercise.

4) If Assisted Living/Memory Care facilities are going to permit patients to have their animals live with them, they need to have a plan in place that involves staff members assuming responsibility for the care of animals that live there.

5) Keeping a dog outside 24/7 is inhumane, and chaining a dog is totally unacceptable.

6) Dogs suffer the consequences of the actions (or in the case of Leon—lack of action) of people.

7) Having the financial resources to put a plan in place (hiring a POA, vet visits, etc.) isn't enough if there's no follow-through and instructions aren't followed.

Everyone involved with Leon before he came to ODH probably thought they were doing the right thing, including Louise, but denial about Leon's physical, mental and emotional condition, and lack of medical care compromised his life in a significant way.

Please think about Leon if you become involved in any way in a similar situation.

Jack

Chapter 25

Dementia

Please take dementia seriously when you're considering your senior dog's quality of life and think very hard about whether it's really in his best interests to just exist instead of living a happy life in which he is fully present.

When I talk with people who are struggling with the decision to let their senior dogs move on to their next expression of spirit the issue of dementia often comes up, but I've found that people are sometimes unwilling to consider euthanasia if the problem isn't physical. Somehow it's easier (well, actually I know it's never easy) to come to terms with the fact that a dog is suffering physically and needs to move on than it is to understand that mental and emotional suffering need to be taken into consideration as well as physical problems. My experiences with my own dogs, as well as many conversations with people about their dogs, has brought me to several thoughts that I'd like to share with you.

1) My bottom line is always **quality of life** when I'm talking with people about end-of-life decisions for their dogs. Dementia is an insidious and relentless condition that is very difficult for a dog to handle ... and for you to deal with if you're the person who loves the dog. Here are some behaviors to look for if you have concerns about your dog's mental/emotional health:

- Pacing, anxiousness, movement that doesn't seem purposeful, disorientation

- Staring for long periods of time, getting lost in corners, standing on the wrong side of a door waiting for it to open, unable to figure out the next step, acting dazed, seeming to be lost in familiar places

- Peeing/pooping in the house: Seniors with dementia may forget to go outside to do their business, but it's important to rule out a medical problem (urinary tract infection, bladder stones, or gastrointestinal problems) before assuming the problem is related to dementia.

- Withdrawing: A dog with dementia often won't seek out human companionship, sometimes will even walk away while being petted, and often won't greet family members when they come home.

- Barking for no reason: The dog may no longer recognize people, or the dog may be lost in the yard or behind a door, or is generally confused ... which could cause barking, especially at night.

- Appetite changes that manifest in either losing interest in food or always being hungry

- Sleeping pattern changes: A dog with dementia may sleep more than normal, or have night and day reversed—sleeping during the day and awake and confused at night.

- Not responsive to your voice : You need to first rule out hearing loss, but if that isn't the problem, the dementia may be interfering with your dog's ability to process what you're saying and act on your request, or the dog may even may be confused about his or her name when you call it.

- Any other behaviors that might be unusual for your dog.

If you notice some of the above signs I'd suggest you keep track of what behaviors you've seen so you can determine how often they're occurring. Then, make an appointment with your vet to discuss what's going on. Your vet may prescribe medications/supplements that can be helpful with dementia in its early stages, but you need to be mindful of the fact that often some medications are aimed at just reducing anxiety and you may end up with a dog that is not only confused, but also tranquilized and barely responsive, which means you're trading one unhealthy state for another.

2) Are you wearing the tee shirt that says *"Denial Isn't Just a River in Egypt"*? If you've read through the above list of common symptoms of dementia you may find yourself trying to explain away any symptoms your dog is experiencing by saying: "He'll be better tomorrow." "She's just having a bad day." "I don't think she really minds being confused; after all, people are confused all the time." "He isn't in pain." Please don't rationalize what's going on mentally or emotionally with your dog. Like people, dogs function on many different levels and like us, they like to be in control of their minds and bodies. Don't compare your senior moments to what your dog is experiencing with dementia. When you walk into a room and forget why you're there that's often a momentary lapse caused by distraction on your part. Or, if you find your socks in the refrigerator, you just laugh and chalk the misplacement up to not paying attention. Your dog isn't laughing when he can't figure out how he got stuck in a corner. And ... dementia is painful on an emotional and mental level.

3) Is the **light** still there in your dog's eyes? I do understand that if your dog is blind or is vision impaired it's difficult to tell whether or not the light is still there, but even with blind dogs you can sense whether the light is or isn't there. The light I'm talking about sometimes isn't so much a tangible thing as it is just a sense that your dog is still in there. If you feel like your dog isn't fully present any longer, and that no one is home, the light is fading or gone.

4) **There's a big difference between existing and living.** Dogs can exist with dementia for a long time, but that existence is without joy, eventually is filled with fear, and can't be called living in any true sense of the word.

5) When your dog **loses his or her sense of identity** that's serious business. Recently I had to say goodbye to one of my dogs that was suffering from dementia. It was heart wrenching to watch him lose his sense of identity because dogs function on an intuitive level most of the time, and their sense of who they are as dogs is important to them. Their sense of identity gives purpose and joy to their lives, and when they become confused about who they are that sense of purpose and joy is compromised.

After reading the above paragraphs I know you must feel helpless and frustrated, but if your dog is in the early stages of dementia and you aren't seeing the above-mentioned behaviors to any significant degree to cause you to consider euthanasia here's what you can do to help:

- Offer your dog reassurance, physical comfort, and a constant reminder that you're there.

- Dementia isn't something a dog should have to deal with alone. Be physically with your dog as much as possible.

- Trust the bond you have with your dog to hold strong. Offer your fully present self to your dog on every level.

- Provide external stimulation (rides in the car, walks, visits to the dog park, playtime with other dogs) to keep the world available to your dog.

- Look for the positive. Allow your dog to see the light in your eyes. Practice being optimistic. <u>Be in the moment with your dog.</u>

- Try whatever your vet might prescribe that won't just drug your dog because often you'll see some good short-term results with the non- tranquilizing meds that will stimulate brain activity. Also, there are several dog foods on the market that claim to help with cognitive dysfunction. In short, with your vet's suggestions in mind, try whatever's out there.

Ok, I've said enough. I'm sure you get my point by now. What I'm talking about here is a steady progression of what I call the "foggy boy" syndrome. What I've found with my own dogs is that initially the confusion and disorientation isn't terribly upsetting to them. They just roll with it and relax into a kind of "It's no big deal; my person will take care of me" state of mind. But, eventually the confusion frightens them, they begin to panic and become fearful. That's no way to live.

Please take dementia seriously when you're considering your senior dog's quality of life and think very hard about whether it's really in his best interests to just exist instead of living a happy life in which he is fully present.

Augustus, Mayor of Whoville

Chapter 26

Making End-of-Life Decisions

*Don't ask him to struggle with a failing body or to stay
too long because you're unwilling to let him go.*

In the last chapter I talked about dementia as a viable consideration when you're facing an end-of-life decision for your dog, but based on the number of inquiries I receive about other conditions that might play into your decision I thought it might be helpful if I expanded the conversation and asked you to look at other issues as well. This is a kind of "big picture" approach to the topic.

Some dogs leave their bodies without assistance from us. Their deaths are "natural" and require no intervention. However, one of the most difficult—yet very necessary—aspects of our responsibility to the dogs we love is sometimes needing to make the decision to allow them to move on to their next expressions of spirit when their bodies or minds fail them, and their quality of life becomes seriously compromised. Our dogs depend on us to help them make their transition, and it's very important to perform that final service for them with love and respect.

Quality of life is the key issue. If your dog is unable to function in a way that assures you that he is still enjoying a good quality of life, then it's time to seriously consider releasing him from his body. Severe incontinence caused by kidney failure, inability to eat, impaired mobility, lack of interest in surroundings, restless movement during sleep often caused by pain, disorientation and confusion, severe vomiting, uncontrollable diarrhea, dementia, failed vision, hearing loss, and the light fading from his eyes are all symptoms that indicate your friend's body and/or mind is failing. If you haven't already done so, make an appointment with your veterinarian to determine the seriousness of the symptoms. Ask for a blood analysis, have x-rays taken if necessary, and in short, have your veterinarian perform whatever diagnostic tests might be helpful. If there is no treatment available to radically alter the symptoms you're seeing, then it's time to release your friend from his body. Within this context, be very careful about having painful treatments or heroic surgery performed on a dog that is suffering. He doesn't deserve to endure more pain just because you don't want him to die. We don't ever want our animal friends to die, but that wanting is unreasonably self-indulgent, and allowing a dog to suffer isn't fulfilling your promise to care for him in all phases of his life. Dogs want to be well, and they want to stay with us as long as they can so you need to be aware of the amount of energy your dog is expending while he is trying to be well. Don't ask him to struggle with a failing body or to stay too long because you're unwilling to let him go.

Don't procrastinate just because the decision you face is a difficult one. Have the strength to do the right thing because you love and respect your animal friend. Indulging in "Maybe he'll be better tomorrow" thoughts only prolongs the inevitable, and will surely invite you to revisit those thoughts with strong feelings of guilt at a later date because you waited too long. Don't look for signs of improvement when they exist only in your hopes. Trust your intuition, and rely on your connection with your animal companion. Put aside your own unwillingness to let your friend go because you will miss him. This time in your animal friend's life is not about you. It's about showing him that you love him enough to release him from his body.

Talk to your dog about your concerns. You've established a pattern of communication with your dog that works for both of you. Let your friend know that you think it may be time for him to move on to his next adventure. Trust that he will hear you and understand that you're ready to release him. Dogs are very loyal and intuitive companions, and if your friend understands that you're ready, he will rest easier knowing that peace will soon come to him because you've heard him and understand that it's time for him to physically leave you. Don't even doubt for one minute that your friend will hear you. Dogs know what we're thinking and feeling — often far better than we do — and your thoughts and feelings will be heard.

Once you've made the decision, **don't second guess yourself.** It's quite common to have second thoughts because ... well, because it's so hard and you really don't want to lose your friend. Or, perhaps once you've made the decision you see what you interpret as improvement in your dog's condition. Be careful here: don't read into what you see just because you so desperately want your dog to be well. Or, you may actually see a bit of change, but that's because your dog knows you've heard him, and is showing you that he's relieved you'll be releasing him from his body. Within this context I once spoke with a woman who was reluctant to let her dog go because she felt like she would be taking his life and in fact, as she said— killing him. I told her that the disease, in this case cancer, was killing her dog's body and that by releasing him from his body she was giving him life, not ending it. Dogs are much more than their bodies. What they are as spirit lives forever.

If you are able to draw on your reserve of strength to make the decision necessary to release your friend from his body, reach inside of yourself one more time and **stay with your dog** after you bring him to the veterinarian to have the injection administered that will send him on his way. (Some veterinarians will come to your home if you'd prefer to have your friend leave in a familiar setting, and if you are able to arrange this, that's the best possible way of saying goodbye.) Regardless of location, your presence is very important at this most difficult time. Being able to hold your dog and feel all of the pain and discomfort slip away is a necessary conclusion to your physical friendship. Ask the veterinarian to sedate your friend so there is absolutely no discomfort involved for either of you.

Understand that death is just change. Certainly you will grieve for the loss of your dog's physical presence, but know that you will always carry the love you shared with your dog in your heart. That permanence of spirit never changes.

Chapter 27

He Knows You're With Him

He leaves his body with a full heart and mind.

Jasper

I've had quite a few conversations with people who were unable to physically be with their dog when the dog died, and they feel guilty and even angry. If you've ever felt the same way I have a few thoughts that might be of help:

I think it's safe to say that most people want to physically be with their dogs when they die. Being able to hold a dog you love as he leaves his body is important and provides a kind of closure. But, due to a variety of circumstances, being there physically isn't always possible. How do you get over feeling guilty for not physically being there?

If you're unable to be physically with your dog—for whatever reason—when he leaves his body it's important to understand that even though you may not physically be present, your thoughts and feelings are there, and your dog knows that. As I've said before, dogs process everything emotionally and intuitively, and your love for your dog exists on more than the physical plane. He can feel your presence. He knows you care. He knows you feel sad. He knows you don't want him to leave. He knows you love him. Trust the connection you have with your dog. That connection isn't broken by dying or even death.

Don't contaminate the grieving process with guilt. Grieving is hard enough without piling guilt on top of it. Playing the "shoulda...woulda...coulda" game only makes it harder to deal with the death of your dog. Dogs don't judge, and you shouldn't waste your time and energy judging yourself either.

I understand that what I'm saying is easier said than done but look at it from a broader perspective. Because of COVID we've been spending time during the past couple of years being physically apart from most people. Does that distancing mean that people don't know what other people are feeling and thinking? When you care, those feelings find their way to those who need to know they aren't alone. Remember the ripple effect. The same process is true of the connection between you and your dog.

Dogs are better at dealing with emotions than we are, but perhaps one of the lessons you've learned from your dog is that feelings are as tangible (and much more important) than thoughts. You can say goodbye in your heart and those feelings will be felt by your dog.

During the time your dog shared your life you taught him that he wasn't alone. It wasn't really a conscious teaching on your part; you showed him in every way you could that you loved him and were there for him. You didn't need to be standing in front of him to get that message across. That same principle applies when he leaves his body.

Here's the bottom line: Trust that how you feel, and everything your dog meant to you exists in your dog's mind and heart when he leaves his body. He won't feel alone if you can't physically be with him because he's had a life with you that filled him with love and taught him he was never alone. He leaves his body with a full heart and mind. His heart is bigger because you've shared yours with him, and yours is bigger because he's shared his heart with you.

Please let go of the guilt and anger. Those feelings get in the way of the grieving that's necessary for you to honor the memory of your dog. Accept what is and understand that your dog knows you're with him when he goes Home regardless of where you are.

Brooke Mallory Photography

Marcia Jean

Chapter 28

Productive Grieving

But it can be productive, and serve as a way for you to honor and validate the importance of a life shared with an animal.

If my use of the word "productive" to describe grieving sounds odd to you, indulge me a bit while I ask you to think about grieving in a way that can be productive.

Grieving, like any emotion, can be productive if you allow yourself to experience the emotions attached to grieving in a way that is helpful to you. I know ... you're thinking that the only thing that would be helpful would be if you still had your animal friend physically with you—healthy and happy. But, whether you're animal or human, living in a body that eventually dies is inevitable, so some degree of acceptance of that reality is the first part of the grieving process. You don't have to like what you need to accept. You just need to do it.

Grieving for your dog is important. All of the feelings that go along with the process honor and validate the importance of your friend's presence in your life. Saying goodbye is difficult, but it should be. Why would it be easy to say goodbye to a well-loved companion? If it were easy to say goodbye, you wouldn't need to grieve.

Even though every situation is different, and we all have to deal with our own sadness and sense of loss, perhaps these thoughts may help you put your grieving energy to positive use:

- Remind yourself that it's your companion's life with you that you want to remember and celebrate, not the end of the physical experience. Do something tangible to honor the life you shared: make a donation in your friend's honor, or perhaps plant a tree or flowers to celebrate your friend's life. Whatever works for you. Just do something positive that specifically honors your friend.

- If you find you have no one to talk with about your friend, sit down and write your loving companion a letter. Actually, this is a good idea even if you do have people to talk with because it's hard to talk and cry at the same time. Allow the words that don't come easily in conversation to find their way to paper. Write down everything you feel. Tell your friend how much he meant to you. Thoughts and feelings have a way of finding their way Home regardless of how they're expressed. Trust me; your friend will hear you.

- If you have pictures of your companion, put together a photo montage. Every picture will conjure up a memory you don't want to lose. This activity can be very therapeutic and reinforce the knowledge that you shared a wonderful life together.

- Take walks in the places you and your companion favored. This is a particularly good healing experience if your friend was ill and not able to walk much toward the end. If you really focus, you'll see your friend bouncing alongside or racing ahead in perfect health. Allow yourself to feel your friend's presence, and know that his spirit is with you.

• Think about everything your friend has taught you. Think about the lessons of pure love, devotion, patience, friendship, intuitive understanding, acceptance, playfulness and joy that you never would have learned if you hadn't been willing to welcome an animal into your life.

• If you have any regrets or "hindsight guilties," put them to rest by understanding that dogs never judge. You don't need to indulge in this senseless activity either. To think all kinds of: "If only I had ... I wish I hadn't ... Why didn't I ...?" thoughts only prolongs your sadness and creates frustration over what can't be changed. Grieving is hard enough without adding guilt to complicate the process. Regardless of the circumstances of your friend's death, know that all of your actions were accepted with understanding and without judgment. If you think your friend left too soon, cherish the quality of your relationship without being sad about a life you feel was too short. Animals live in the moment, and it's important you believe every moment you shared with your friend was significant.

• Understand that death means nothing to an animal. It's just change. The death of your friend's body allows your companion to move on to his or her next expression of spirit. What matters is that you know you've sent your friend Home with love, and that forever kind of love defies any boundaries or limitations of time and space. I suppose it's a cliché to say that your friend will always be with you in spirit, but I believe that to be true. There's a place in your heart reserved for every animal you've ever loved. Instead of thinking that your heart is broken, think of your heart as being bigger because your dog shared his heart with you.

143

- Finally, please don't say that you'll never have another dog in your life because dealing with the death of an animal friend is too hard. To make this kind of pronouncement does a great dishonor to your friend, and never allows you to use what you've learned from your companion. There are so many animals wherever you are as you read this that would welcome the opportunity to love and be loved. Visit your nearby shelter and see who might be there just waiting for you. Allow another animal to touch your heart. You'll know when you're ready. And when you are, don't be surprised if you sense a familiar voice whispering "Go on, pick him. You're gonna love her. I'll bet he likes to play ball too. She needs you. Share our love with your new friend."

Grieving is never an enjoyable process. It's hard. It's painful. It's exhausting. But it can be productive, and serve as a way for you to honor and validate the importance of a life shared with an animal. Be strong and allow yourself this necessary emotional experience.

Chapter 29

I Loved You, If Only for a Moment

For a sick (physical, mental or emotional) dog to feel the love of a human—even for a short time—is a powerful message.

Banjo

I think one of the most important services of love we offer at Old Dog Haven is to provide hospice care for dogs that are only with us a short time. We can do this because we have foster families who understand what their role is with the dog that can't be with them very long. This belief is underlined by one of our dedicated foster moms, and I just wanted to emphasize her message.

"Sometimes our role is simply to be here to help set another soul free with love, dignity and compassion ... and as part of a family. It was an honor to be of service and see you set free from your pain and suffering. You will always be in our hearts, lovely man."

I know that those of us who take in senior dogs hope they come to us for rehabilitation, and with Old Dog Haven's financial assistance, we very often can help them and improve the quality of their lives. In many cases this kind of transformation does happen. However, sometimes our role in a dog's life isn't that of rehab cheerleader but rather we need to be the person who provides loving hospice care and then releases the dog from his body even if the dog was only with us a short period of time—hours, days, weeks. I once took in a dog that was only with me for six hours. My role in his life was not rehab-cheerleader, but I was the person who needed to let him go because no one else would. Many of us who are fosters for Old Dog Haven have had similar experiences: I've known our director of veterinary services to sit up all night holding a dog that needed to feel loved and valued before she released him from his body. Some of you can add your own experiences here.

I think of dogs as messengers; they come to us with messages and lessons for us to learn, and they also return Home with messages and lessons they learned while they were with us. For a sick (physical, mental or emotional) dog to feel the love of a human—even for a short time—is a powerful message. Because dogs live in the moment, how we feel about them, even if they can't be physically with us for long, stays with them and is a hopeful message about humans that the dog delivers when he returns Home.

Harry Pawter

Chapter 30

I Don't Know what to Say

Reaching out is a good thing; just know your audience and be sincere, regardless of what you say or do.

If you know someone who has had to say goodbye to their dog, do you struggle with what to say to them? I'm asking because over the years I've had quite a few people talk with me about this concern, and they've asked me to write about it so I thought I'd throw out a few thoughts that might help.

1) Know your audience: If the person grieving is someone you know really well, and you also knew the dog, you might talk about memories you have of the dog ... "I remember the time he ..." When you refer to the dog, that reminiscence tells your friend that you had a connection with the dog too, and might help relieve some of the isolation the person feels. On the other hand, if you're just reading a post on Facebook and you don't really know the person and didn't know the dog, a simple "I'm sorry." might be enough.

2) Be careful about saying, "I know exactly how you feel" because that might be presumptuous on your part. You may have had the same experience, but everyone grieves in their own way and launching into an account about how you felt when you went through the same thing might not be helpful, and it might create the impression that you're more interested in talking about yourself than expressing sympathy.

3) Try not to offer suggestions about how to deal with the loss before you ask if the person would like some suggestions. We sometimes think our advice is always needed when in fact many people just need to vent and aren't looking for suggestions.

4) Speak from your heart. If you're feeling sad for the person, then just simply say "My heart goes out to you" or something similar. Your sincerity will come through.

5) Think about what you might want (or would have liked) people to say to you in the same circumstance and go from there.

6) Saying nothing doesn't really feel right. If you feel like you want/need to express your feelings to the grieving person, don't cop out by not saying anything. This is particularly true if you know the person. Pretending that someone hasn't experienced the death of a dog by talking about everything but that is artificial and comes off as being insensitive, and the grieving person will feel even more isolated than they already do.

7) Saying "Don't cry." doesn't help. Tears are a necessary part of the grieving process. Just because you're uncomfortable with someone else's tears doesn't mean that crying isn't a necessary action for them.

8) You might want to ask "How can I help you?" This question then gives the person an opening to talk about what they need from you. If they say that they don't need anything from you, you need to accept that, and just let them know you're there for them if they need you.

9) Do something nice: bring flowers, plant a tree or shrub in memory of the dog in your friend's yard, or make a donation in the dog's memory.

10) "You need to get another dog" might not be the right thing to say. Yet. The length of time it takes for someone to welcome a new dog into their home and heart after their dog friend has died varies and you can't rush the process. Some people are ready right away but others often take a longer period of time. Honor the process.

Bottom line? Reaching out is a good thing; just know your audience and be sincere, regardless of what you say or do.

Soren

Chapter 31

End Notes

Because of the love you shared with your dog, your heart is bigger. It's not broken.

Buoy

So, what's your takeaway from the thoughts I've presented in the book? Hopefully you learned a few things that you found helpful, smiled on occasion, found a kindred spirit in my perspective, were inspired to adopt or foster, and ... you can supply whatever else might be on your mind.

There are a couple of points that I hope made sense to you as you read:

1) Dogs live in the moment, so it's very important to be in the moment with them. As I look back through previous chapters I notice that I mentioned this idea in one way or another at least six times. The repetition is deliberate because if you don't take away anothing else from this book, this is the idea that I think is not only most important, but most helpful. If you get this, and can do it you'll really notice a difference in the quality of the time you share with your dog. If you understand that often the past and future contaminate today, you'll enhance today by being fully present.

2) I'd also like you to think about what I said with regard to not feeling sorry for your dog. Your senior dog—regardless of how he came to you—needs your positive thoughts and feelings rather than your sympathy. Again, I'm not suggesting that you don't let him know that you're sorry about his past, or whatever is going on with him now, but the focus should be on your positive relationship with each other. If you let him, your dog will help you find joy where you least expect it.

3) Also, please think about the ripple effect idea. I know that there are so many dogs in the world that need help it's sometimes overwhelming to think about what needs to be done for them, but just know that whatever you do to help sends a message out into the ozone, and that message is received by those dogs in need. Yes, one person can make a difference. One hug. One smile. One adoption. These thoughts and actions create positive energy.

4) When it's time for your canine friend to leave you, please don't say that your heart is broken. Because of the love you shared with your dog, your heart is bigger. It's not broken.

Your dog's animal heart has joined your human heart, and it doesn't get any better than that. While it's true that your dog's physical presence is no longer with you, his spirit (you use whatever word here works for you) will always be with you. Always.

5) Finally, give your senior dog opportunities to wear flowers!

Thanks for letting me share my thoughts with you. Hopefully you'll join me in my next book, Listen to Your Inner Dog: Conversations About Being Human, and we'll talk about what's so difficult about being a human being, and how your "inner dog" can help you be a better human.

Pearl

About Pearl, the Cover dog

Pearl came to Julie Austin (cover photographer) in 2008 from Saving Great Animals. The moment Julie saw her she knew they were meant to be together.

Julie says, "Pearl was my Buddha dog. There was not one mean bone in her body. I've never known such an incredibly sweet dog, and I have known many dogs. We had a wonderful 14 years together. She was even sweet upon her death as she passed away in her sleep right next to me. She saved me from having to make that decision for her. I hope that everyone has at least one "Pearl" in their life."

About the Author

Ardeth De Vries's life has gone to the dogs, and she wouldn't have it any other way.

De Vries is a retired teacher, writer, and animal welfare advocate whose work with dogs includes: over 20 years of volunteering at an animal shelter, 55 years of rescuing homeless senior dogs, and the operation (since 2000) of her own nonprofit organization created to assist people who live on Whidbey Island with veterinary expenses for their companion animals. She has also been featured in A Better World Starts Here: Activists and their Work, (Stacy Russo, Sanctuary Publishers, 2019). De Vries has been involved for the past 18 years with Old Dog Haven, the largest senior dogs rescue in the United States. As part of the Old Dog Haven organization De Vries has served as: permanent foster parent, newsletter editor, blog mistress, counselor to people (not only within the organization but all over the U.S.) about end-of-life decisions, grieving, dementia, and senior dog care, transporter, board member, board president, and executive director (retired). De Vries has also been interviewed on radio and T.V. about her work with senior dogs.

De Vries has written two books about dogs and a metaphysical novel that slipped in there between the two dog books:

Animal Voices in Concert, Publishing Works, 2006

A Space Between, River Sanctuary Publishing, 2010

Old Dog Haven: Every Old Dog Has a Story to Tell, Bennett & Hastings, 2014.

De Vries shares her home on Whidbey Island with her partner and five senior rescue dogs. She is currently working on her next book:

Listen to Your Inner Dog: Conversations About Being Human.

All proceeds earned by the author from this book will be donated to Old Dog Haven.

Additional Resources

Keelin

ORGANIZATIONS AND PROGRAMS IN THE UNITED STATES

NATIONAL ANIMAL-WELFARE ASSOCIATIONS

American Humane Association
1400 16th St. NW, #360
Washington, DC 20036
Website: www.americanhumane.org
Phone: 800-227-4645
Email: info@americanhumane.org

American Society for the Prevention of Cruelty to Animals (ASPCA)
424 E. 92nd St.
New York, NY 10128
Website: www.aspca.org
Phone: 888-666-2279
Email: publicinformation@aspca.org

Humane Society of the United States

2100 L St. NW
Washington, DC 20037
Website: www.humanesociety.org
Phone: 202-452-1100 or 866-720-2676

Contact form (Animal Rescue Team)
website: www.humanesociety.org/forms/
contact_us/disaster_services_contact.html

Petfinder

Senior Pet Adoptions - Petfinder

Senior Dogs Project

Extensive clearinghouse of online information to help older dogs.
Website: www.srdogs.com

Susie's Senior Dogs

Facilitates senior-dog adoptions across the United States.
Website: www.susiesseniordogs.com
Facebook page: www.facebook.com/susiesseniordogs
Email: susie.doggie@gmail.com

The Grey Muzzle Organization

Funding and resources helps senior dogs at animal shelters,
rescues, sanctuaries, and other non-profit groups nationwide.

14460 Falls of Neuse Road Suite 149-269
Raleigh, NC 27614
Email: info@greymuzzle.org
Phone:(919) 529-0309

Cowbelle

Moira

Scooby

ORGANIZATIONS AND PROGRAMS BY STATE THAT HELP SENIOR DOGS

ALABAMA

Shelby Humane

381 McDow Rd.
Colombiana, Alabama 35051
Website: https://www.shelbyhumane.org/senior-paws
Phone: 205-669-3916
Email: info@shelbyhumane.org

ALASKA

Loving Companions Animal Rescue's Senior Pets for Senior People Program

1360 Old Richardson Hwy.
North Pole, AK 99705
Website: www.lovingcompanionsanimalrescue.org
Phone: 907-488-0516 or 907-347-4829

Grand Paws Retirement Acres, Inc.

P.O. Box 799
Delta Junction, AK 99737
Website: www.grandpawsretirementacres.com
Email: grandpawsretirementacres@gmail.com

ARIZONA

Forever Loved Pet Sanctuary

P.O. Box 12142
Scottsdale, AZ 85267
Website: www.foreverlovedpetsanctuary.org

Rusty's Angels Sanctuary

P.O. Box 74031
Phoenix, AZ 85007
Website: www.rustysangelssanctuary.org
Email: rustysangelssanctuary@gmail.com
Phone: 480-350-0251

Cherished Tails Senior Sanctuary

PO Box 631
Marana, AZ 85653
Website: www.cherishedtailsseniorsanctuary.weebly.com
Email: cherishedtails@yahoo.com
Phone: 520.616.0171

ARKANSAS

Old Man's River Front Rescue

West Fork, Arkansas
Email: oldmansriverfrontrescue@yahoo.com
Website: http://oldmansriverfrontrescue.weebly.com/

CALIFORNIA

Lily's Legacy Senior Dog Sanctuary

PO Box 751002
Petaluma, CA 94975
Website: www.lilyslegacy.org
Phone: 415-488-4984
Email: lilyslegacysds@gmail.com

Lionel's Legacy

232 Murray Dr.
El Cajon, CA 92020
Website: www.lionelslegacy.org
Phone: 619-212-5623
Email: seniors@lionelslegacy.org

Tails of Gray Senior Dog Rescue

P.O. Box 104
Livermore, CA 94550
Website: www.tailsofgray.org
Phone: 925-286-0468
Email: info@tailsofgray.org

Muttville Senior Dog Rescue

PO Box 410207
San Francisco, CA 94141
Website: www.muttville.org
Phone: 415-272-4172
Email (general): info@muttville.org
Email (Seniors for Seniors Program):
seniorsforseniors@muttville.org

Frosted Faces Foundation

1440 Pine St.
Ramona, CA 92065
Website: www.frostedfacesfoundation.org
Email: info@frostedfacesfoundation.org
Phone: 715-574-6320

COLORADO

Old Dog House

3457 Highland Meadows Dr.
Florissant, CO 80816
Website: www.olddoghousecolorado.org

Izzy's Place Senior Dog Rescue

1261 E. Magnolia St. Unit D #337
Fort Collins, CO 80524
Website: Izzysplaceseniordogrescue.org
Phone: 970.325-3180
Email: Nicolerescue@gmail.com

CONNECTICUT

Out to Pasture Farm & Rescue

PO Box 310174
Newington, CT 06131
Website: www.outtopasture.org
Email: carrie@outtopasture.org

DELAWARE

Senior Dog Haven & Hospice

PO Box 1441
Wilmington, DE 19899
Website: www.seniordoghaven.org
Email: info@seniordoghaven.org

FLORIDA

Paws 4 You Rescue's Seniors Program

PO Box 561163
Miami, FL 33256
Website (Seniors Program): www.paws4you.org/seniors
Email: seniors@paws4you.org

Senior Paws Sanctuary

1413 Caywood Circle S.
Lehigh, FL 33936
Website: http://seniorpawssanctuary.com/
Phone: 239-470-7022
Email: Seniorpsanctuary@aol.com

Roland Senior Dog Rescue Gang

5435 Painted Pony Ave
Melrose, FL 32666
Website: www.rolandrescuegang.com
Phone: 352.256.0286

Sadie

Pasta & Rigatoni

GEORGIA

Frankie and Andy's Place

653 Gainsville Highway
Winder, GA 30690
Website: www.frankieandandysplace.og
Email: info@frankieandandysplace.org

HAWAII

Rainbow Friends Animal Sanctuary

PO Box 1259
17-382 13 Mile Rd.
Kurtistown, HI 96760
Website: www.rainbowfriends.org
Phone: 808-982-5110
Email: mail@rainbowfriends.org

IDAHO

Nash's Forever Haus Sanctuary for Senior/Hospice Dogs

411 E Locust Ln,
Nampa, ID 83686
Website: www.foreverhouse.org
Phone:(208) 720-3897

ILLINOIS

Pets for Seniors

PO Box 64
Edwards, IL 61528
Website: www.petsforseniors.org
Phone: 309-446-9721
Email: pfsshelter@gmail.com

Young at Heart Pet Rescue

PO Box 1293
Palatine, IL 60078
Website: www.adoptaseniorpet.com
Phone: 847-529-2025

Helping Paws Animal Sanctuary Senior to Senior

250 Harding Lane
Woodstock, IL 60098
Website: www. Helping Paws.net/senior-t-senior
Phone: 815-338-4406
Email: info@helpingpaws.net

Lizzy's Fund

Resource for assistance in caring for senior dogs.

INDIANA

Taffy's Touch Senior Dog Rescue

Greenwood, Indiana 46143
Website: www.taffystouchrescue.com
Email: nikki.taffystouchrescue@gmail.com

IOWA

Silver Paw Senior Pets- Animal Rescue League of Iowa

5452 NE 22nd St.
Des Moines, IA 50313
Website: arl-iowa.org

Silver Paw Senior Pets Animal Rescue League of Iowa

Phone: (515) 473-9101
Email: arl-iowa.org

LOUISIANA

Animal Rescue New Orleans

271 Plauche St.
New Orleans, LA 70123
Website: www.animalrescueneworleans.org
Phone (voice mail): 504-571-1900
Email: arnovolunteer@yahoo.com

MARYLAND

Senior Dog Sanctuary

8336 W B & A Rd.
Severm MD 21144
Phone: 443-742-0270
Website: Senior Dog Sanctuary

House with a Heart Senior Pet Sanctuary

6409 Stream Valley Way
Gaithersburg, MD 20882
Website: www.housewithaheart.com
Phone: 240-631-1743
Email: housewithaheart@comcast.net

MINNESOTA

Grey Face Rescue & Retirement

PO Box 7072
St. Cloud, MN 56302
Website: www.greyfacerescue.org
Phone: 952-261-7178
Email: greyfacerescue@gmail.com

MISSISSIPPI

Coco's House Senior Sanctuary and Rescue

PO Box 721314
Byram, MS 39272
Website: https://cocoshouserescue.org/

MISSOURI

Senior Dogs 4 Seniors

1109 Babler Forest Ct.
Chesterfield, MO 63005
Website: www.seniordogs4seniors.com
Phone: 636-458-1892
Email: info@seniordogs4seniors.com

St. Louis Senior Dog Project

7488 Rivermont Trail
House Springs, MO 63051
Website: www.stlsdp.org
Phone: 636-671-7223

Shep's Place Senior Dog Sanctuary

17012 E Truman Rd,
Independence, MO 64056
Website: www.shepsplace.org
(816) 786-8664

MONTANA

Rolling Dog Ranch Animal Sanctuary

400 Rolling Dog Ranch Ln.
Ovando, MT 59854
Website: www.rollingdogranch.com

Phone: 406-793-6000
Email: info@rollingdogranch.org

Tails as Old as Time

121 E. Corcoran Street
Lewistown, MT 59457
Website: www.tailsasoldastime.org
Phone: 406-366-3200

NEVADA

Homer J's Senior Dog Sanctuary

420 Reno Ave.
Reno, NV 89503
Website: http://www.seniordogsanctuary.org/

NEW HAMPSHIRE

Libby's Haven for Senior Canines

A P. O. Box 65,
Canterbury, NH 03224
Website: http://www.LHSK9.org
Phone: 603.783.9416
Email: lhsk9@comcast.net

NEW JERSEY

Monkey's House: A Dog Hospice & Sanctuary

P.O. Box 2332
Vincentown, NJ 08088
Website: www.monkeyshouse.org

Marty's Place Senior Dog Sanctuary

118 Route 526
Upper Freehold Township, NJ 08501
Website: www.martysplace.org
Phone: 609-259-1278
Email: info@martysplace.org

NEW MEXICO

Sunflower Sanctuary Animal Rescue

25 Clauss Place
Tijeras, NM 87059
Email: sunflowersanctuary@msn.com
Phone: 505-286-16302

NORTH CAROLINA

Forever Dreams Senior Dog Sanctuary

Tryon NC
Phone: 828-817-0859
Email: foreverdreamsds@gmail.com

OHIO

Sanctuary for Senior Dogs

PO Box 609054
Cleveland, OH 44109
Website: www.sanctuaryforseniordogs.org
Phone: 216-485-9233

OREGON

Senior Dog Rescue of Oregon

PO Box 1051
Philomath, OR 97370
Website: www.sdroregon.com
Phone: 541-224-2488
Email: SDROregon@gmail.com

PENNSYLVANIA

Mureille's Place- A Senior Dog Sanctuary

533 Creek Rd.
Wapwallopen, Pa 18660
Phone: 570-579-8172
Email: info@mureillesplace.org

Senior Pet and Animal Rescue

PO Box 99751
Pittsburgh, PA 15233

TENNESSEE

Old Friends Senior Dog Sanctuary

PO Box 93
Mount Juliet, TN 37121
Website: www.ofsds.org
Email: ofsdstn@gmail.com

Willy's Happy Endings

2073 Wilma Rudolph Blvd.
Clarksville, TN 37040
Website: www.willyshappyendings.org
Phone: 931-217-4495
Email: WillysRescue@gmail.com

UTAH

Best Friends Animal Sanctuary

5001 Angel Canyon Rd.
Kanab, UT 84741
Website: www.bestfriends.org/sanctuary
Phone: 435-644-2001
Email: info@bestfriends.org

Best Friends Animal Society–Utah

2005 S. 1100 East
Salt Lake City, UT 84106
Website: utah.bestfriends.org
Phone: 801-574-2454
Email: utahpets@bestfriends.org

VIRGINIA

Richmond Animal League's Seniors for Seniors Program

11401 International Dr.
Richmond, VA 23236
Website: www.ral.org
Phone: 804-379-0046
Email: adopt@ral.org

Old Dog Haven

P.O. Box 1409
Oak Harbor, WA 98277
Website: www.olddoghaven.org
Phone: 206.280.7614
email: office@olddoghaven.org

Bella & Gunther

www.ingramcontent.com/pod-product-compliance
Lightning Source LLC
Chambersburg PA
CBHW051212090426
42742CB00021B/3428